CHINA 2014
The Year in Books

CHINA 2014 : THE YEAR IN BOOKS
ISBN 978-988-13642-1-0

© 2014 *The Asian Review of Books*

Published by Chameleon Press Ltd. for *The Asian Review of Books*
15/F, 1506-7 Pacific Plaza, 418 Des Voeux Road West, Hong Kong
www.chameleonpress.com
www.asianreviewofbooks.com

Published in Hong Kong

The Asian Review of Books

www.asianreviewofbooks.com
apps for iPhone and iPad
twitter: @BookReviewsAsia

Editor: Peter Gordon
Chair of the Editorial Board: Mark Clifford

This print edition contains selections published electronically on *asianreviewofbooks.com* between January and November 2014. Some may have been been edited for print. All rights reserved. No part of this book may be reproduced in any form or by any electronic means, including information storage and retrieval systems, without permission in writing from the publisher. Except as otherwise noted, where excerpts have been republished with permission, all materials are copyright *The Asian Review of Books*.

Opinions expressed herein are those of the reviewer/writer and do not necessarily reflect the opinions of *The Asian Review of Books*.

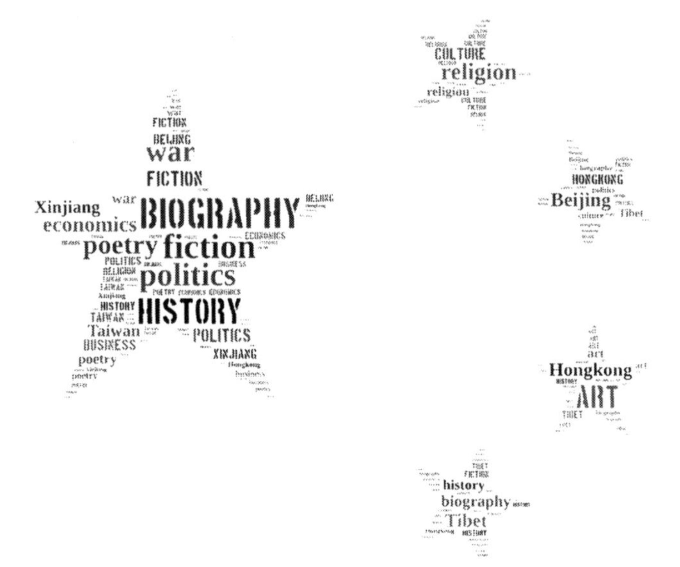

CHINA 2014
The Year in Books

From the Editor:

TO COMPILE A BOOK of book reviews might be, to use what seems to be the *mot du jour*, archetypally "meta". But unlike single articles, grouping several dozen reviews on a single topic provides a unique overview as well as a built-in bibliography.

China 2014 is designed as a broad-brush introduction to the diversity and depth of what is being written in and about China, Taiwan and Hong Kong. While fiction, travel-writing and books on Chinese history, politics, international relations and business are to be expected, these have also included collections of essays, memoir, literary criticism, China's relations with India and Africa, Christianity in China, urbanization, the environment, language and even alcohol and Bitcoin.

The new fiction ranges from children's books to everything from crime to literary fiction, both in translation and that written originally in English. We end with a few volumes of poetry.

Finally, the books include those published in Hong Kong, China and India as well as those from multinational and academic publishers in America and Britain.

This collection isn't meant to be definitive. How could it be? There are many times more books published—even on the single, albeit huge, subject of China—for any publication to be able to cover them all. It will miss books that many readers will no doubt think should have been reviewed, but it will also include a number of books that some readers will otherwise not have come across.

Peter Gordon, Editor
Hong Kong, 1 December 2014

The Year in Non-Fiction

Kerry Brown

HOW WILL WE remember 2014 for what it told us about the aspirations, hope and ambitions of China? Will we see it as part of the revelatory path as the country ascends to global dominance, heading toward what its leader Xi Jinping referred to as the "centennial goals"—the hundredth anniversary of the foundation of the Communist Party, and the achievement of middle income status in 2021? Will it be the year in which "the China Dream" Xi first spoke of back in December 2013 finally became clearer to the world, and the world started dreaming the same things in the same way as China? Or will it figure as a moment of light when China seemed to be poised for greater things before its economic, political, social and environmental issues finally closed in and killed off these dreams?

This is a collection which celebrates the diversity of China—seen from outside, and from inside, a China seen through its history, its culture and literature, its people and their stories, by the authors of the books here, and the reviewers who responded to them. How many countries could have inspired this rich response? Whatever we say about China in 2014, it was not a tepid, emotionless subject. It inspired passionate responses, ideas, reactions. Sometimes these were fearful. Sometimes full of hope. More often than not they carried many questions.

Xi Jinping sits at the center of this, a Chinese leader who captured the imagination in more ways than his predecessors, and who at least started to map out what a world where China figured larger and more confident might look like. China under him was willing to reach into the resources of its immense past, and to speak from its own diversity, to a world where its impact was felt from Africa, to Australia, to America and Latin America. It was a China pushing boundaries, reaching into the lives of the world around it and beyond in ways which would have been hard to envisage even a decade before.

Working out where this China might be heading necessarily involved having an idea of where it had come from. This accounts for the many excellent treatments reviewed in this collection of China's modern past, and stories from even farther back. Many of these recounted tales that had an eerie resonance with today—foreigners getting embroiled in the country's internal affairs, sometimes doing good, sometimes bad, but always recording a fascination with the complexity, magic and wonder of a China that never were often never finally able to pin down.

Hopefully that wonder will carry from the reviewers in this collection to a wider readership. China's fundamental importance, whether we are talking about the differences of Tibet, the turbulence in Hong Kong through 2014, the vexed politics of Taiwan, or China's sometimes brittle relations with its neighbor, is only doubted by the most recalcitrant purblind these days.

Getting the modern world right means getting China right in that vision of the world. That is why thinking hard about the issues raised in this diverse collection is important. Hilary Clinton may well have claimed that the US was the necessary country. But China has fast become the unavoidable one. Thinking about the world means thinking about China. And this book is a great place to start doing that.

The Year in Literature

Marysia Juszczakiewicz

FOR NEARLY A DECADE, I have agented Chinese fiction in translation. It has been interesting and frequently surprising to me to see which titles sell overseas and how they are are received by their new readership.

Chinese fiction has recently been riding a wave in terms of its global audience, with an increase in the variety of stories, genres and voices now available in English translation. But first a word of caution: frequently the success of a Chinese author overseas is gauged by the number of countries in which they are translated, rather than actual units sold.

Perhaps one of the most significant recent developments has been the proliferation of crime stories, banned under Mao since officially crime did not exist. Post-Mao there has been an abundance of works focusing on wrongdoing and corruption, offering trenchant, often challenging insights into modern-day China.

This year, for instance, saw the publication of Mai Jia's *Decoded*, a literary thriller about cryptology in the 1950s, which has now been sold in over twenty languages. He Jiahong's *Black Holes*, written by a law professor in Beijing and published by Penguin China, offers an authoritative insight into the contemporary legal system.

Another interesting development has been the sale of translation rights in popular Chinese science fiction such as the first in Liu Cixin's "Three Body Trilogy", *The Three Body Problem*.

Established literary names such as Nobel Prizewinner Mo Yan will always find a Western audience. His most recent novel *Frog* translated by Howard Goldblatt explores the one-child policy, a topic also treated with black humor by Liu Zhenyun in *I Did Not Kill My Husband*. There were similarly politically sensitive stories from Chan Koonchung, *The Unbearable World of Champa the Driver*, translated by Nicky Harman, offering an unflinching examination of Sino-Tibetan relations, and Chen Xiwo, whose *Book of Sins* exposes the decay within Chinese society today.

There are lighter, more quirky works too, such as Han Dong's *The Tabby Cat's Tale*, as well as tales of contemporary China like *White Horse* by Yan Ge and *Running Through Beijing* by Xu Zechen translated by Eric Abrahamsen.

From the other Chinese-speaking territories, Taiwan's Wu Ming-yi's *The Man with the Compound Eyes* is a compelling story of magical realism, while Singapore's Yeng Pway Ngon *Trivialities about Me and Myself* and Hong Kong's Dorothy Tse's collection of magic realist stories, *Snow and Shadows*, have also found a readership in translation.

Of course, not every great story about China originates there. Notable books written in English range from a novel based on Ming Dynasty artist Wang Meng, *The Ten Thousand Things* by John Spurling, to Ken Bridgewaters's *Open Verdict*, a true-life story based around an unsolved murder in Hong Kong, and Duncan Jepson's *Emperors Once More*, a thriller set against the threat of international financial meltdown.

There is a real drive to present Chinese stories on different platforms, be it in other languages or different media. The major US film studios, for instance, are busily scouting for the definitive "China Story", which will transcend cultural barriers. But to answer the question I am most frequently asked—When will a Chinese blockbuster go global and sell in substantial numbers, East and West?—I have to say, one day... but perhaps not quite yet.

Contributors

Kerry Brown is Director of the China Studies Centre at the University of Sydney, Professor of Chinese Politics, and Team Leader of the Europe China Research and Advice Network. His most recent book is *The New Emperors: Power and the Party in China.*

Agnès Bun is a French reporter based in Hong Kong. She won the Daniel Pearl Award in 2010.

John Butler is Associate Professor of Humanities at the University College of the North in The Pas, Manitoba, Canada, and has taught at universities in Canada, Nigeria and Japan. He specializes in early modern travel-literature (especially Asian travel) and seventeenth-century intellectual history. His latest book is an edition of *Sir Thomas Herbert's Travels in Africa, Persia and Asia the Great* (2012).

Jonathan Chatwin is a British writer who has lived in, and written on, China. He is the author of *Anywhere Out of the World: The Work of Bruce Chatwin.*

Mark L. Clifford is the author of the forthcoming *The Greening of Asia* (Columbia University Press, 2015). He is the executive director of the Asia Business Council.

Nigel Collett is the author of *The Butcher of Amritsar: Brigadier-General Reginald Dyer* and *Firelight of a Different Colour*, about Hong Kong actor Leslie Cheung.

Gianni Criveller, a long time Hong Kong resident, is a historian and religious scholar. He has authored numerous essays and books on the reception of Christianity in China, including (in collaboration) *500 Years of Italians in Hong Kong & Macau* (2013).

Sinead Ferris is a Junior Policy Associate at the University of Sydney's China Studies Centre and Editor of *Emerging Scholars*, the Australian Institute of International Affairs's peer-reviewed journal for young researchers.

Nicholas Gordon, originally from Hong Kong and a recent graduate of Harvard, is an MPhil candidate at Oxford in International Relations. His writing has also appeared in *The South China Morning Post*, *The Diplomat*, *China Daily* and elsewhere.

Peter Gordon is editor of *The Asian Review of Books*.

Coraline Goron is a PhD Candidate in Political Science at ULB (Belgium) and Warwick University (UK) and associate at the European Institute for Asian Studies.

Tim Hannigan is an author and journalist specializing in Indonesia and the Indian Subcontinent. His most recent book, *Raffles and the British Invasion of Java*, is an account of the five-year British interregnum in nineteenth-century Java, and won the 2013 John Brooks Award.

Melanie Ho chairs the Hong Kong Writers Circle. She has reviewed for publications in Hong Kong and Canada.

Jane Houng is a Hong Kong-based writer of children's fiction, including the young adult novel, *Bloodswell* and three chapter books, as well as a biography and educational material.

Marysia Juszczakiewicz is the founder and owner of Peony Literary Agency and has extensive experience of publishing in both the UK and Asia. She has successfully sold many works in Asia. Peony was the the first agent to represent the recent Nobel Prize winner Mo Yan and sold English language rights for his novel *Sandalwood Death*.

Henry Wei Leung is the author of *Paradise Hunger* (Swan Scythe Press, 2012). He maintained a column on contemporary Asian American poetics at the Lantern Review, which is currently on hiatus. He earned his degrees from Stanford and the University of Michigan, and has received Kundiman, Soros, and Fulbright fellowships, among several awards. He is currently in Hong Kong doing research and finishing some books.

Loh Su Hsing is an Assistant Director in the Communications Group at the Prime Minister's Office (Singapore). She holds a PhD in International Relations from Fudan University.

Rosie Milne runs *Asian Books Blog*. She lives in Singapore.

Juan José Morales writes for the Spanish magazine *Compromiso Empresarial*. A former President of the Spanish Chamber of Commerce in Hong Kong, he has a Master of International and Public Affairs from the University of Hong Kong and has also studied international relations at Peking University (Beida).

Tim O'Connell is a China trader turned writer and historian who has lived in Hong Kong and Beijing since 1981.

Angelo Paratico is an Italian journalist living in Hong Kong. He is author of several books in Italian and English, the most recent of which is *Nero: An Exemplary Life*.

Bill Purves is a Hong Kong-based writer. He is the author of several books, including *A Sea of Green: A Voyage Around the World of Ocean Shipping* and *China on the Lam: On Foot Across the People's Republic*.

John D. Van Fleet is Assistant Dean for the USC-SJTU Global Executive MBA in Shanghai. His book, *Tales of Old Tokyo*, a romp through the city's history from 1853 to 1964, will be published in late 2014.

Jennifer Wong is a Hong Kong poet now residing in London. Her most recent book is *Goldfish*.

John W. W. Zeiser is a freelance writer based in Los Angeles. His criticism and poetry has appeared or is forthcoming in a number of publications.

Contents

Non-fiction

Meltdown in Tibet: China's Reckless Destruction of Ecosystems from the Highlands of Tibet to the Deltas of Asia by Michael Buckley
reviewed by Sinead Ferris 2

Chinese Rules: Mao's Dog, Deng's Cat, and Five Timeless Lessons from the Front Lines in China by Tim Clissold
reviewed by Peter Gordon 6

City of Darkness Revisited by Greg Girard and Ian Lambot
reviewed by Mark L. Clifford 9

From the Tsar's Railway to the Red Army: The Experience of Chinese Labourers in Russia during the First World War and Bolshevik Revolution by Mark O'Neill
reviewed by Juan José Morales 12

Living Karma: The Religious Practices of Ouyi Zhixu by Beverley Foulks McGuire
reviewed by John Butler 15

Picnics Prohibited: Diplomacy in a Chaotic China During the First World War by Frances Wood
reviewed by Peter Gordon 19

Chinese Comfort Women: Testimonies from Imperial Japan's Sex Slaves by Peipei Qiu, with Su Zhiliang and Chen Lifei
reviewed by Jonathan Chatwin 21

Villages in the City: South China's Informal Settlements and *Factory Towns of South China*, edited by Stefan Al; *Paris Reborn* by Stephane Kirkland
reviewed by Mark L. Clifford 24

The South China Sea by Bill Hayton and *Fire on the Water: China, America, and the Future of the Pacific* by Robert Haddick
reviewed by Peter Gordon 29

I Stand Corrected: How Teaching Western Manners in China Became Its Own Unforgettable Lesson by Eden Collinsworth
reviewed by Melanie Ho 34

Strangers Across the Border: Indian Encounters in Boomtown China
by Reshma Patil
reviewed by Nicholas Gordon 38

Chomping at the Bitcoin: The Past, Present and Future of Bitcoin in China
by Zennon Kapron
reviewed by Peter Gordon 41

By All Means Necessary: How China's Resource Quest is Changing the World by Elizabeth C. Economy and Michael Levi
reviewed by Loh Su Hsing 44

The Opium War: Drugs, Dreams and the Making of China by Julia Lovell
reviewed by Peter Gordon 47

The Emperor Far Away: Travels at the Edge of China by David Eimer
reviewed by Tim Hannigan 52

Eastern Fortress: A Military History of Hong Kong, 1840-1970 b
y Kwong Chi Man and Tsoi Yiu Lun
reviewed by Bill Purves 57

Betrayal in Paris: How the Treaty of Versailles Led to China's Long Revolution by Paul French
reviewed by Peter Gordon 60

The Mongol Empire: Genghis Khan, His Heirs and the Founding of Modern China by John Man
reviewed by Peter Gordon 63

Tibet: An Unfinished Story
by Lezlee Brown Halper and Stefan Halper
reviewed by Sinead Ferris 67

Getting Stuck in for Shanghai: Putting the Kibosh on the Kaiser from the Bund; The British at Shanghai and the Great War by Robert Bickers
reviewed by Peter Gordon 70

Age of Ambition: Chasing Fortune, Truth and Faith in the New China
by Evan Osnos
reviewed by Jonathan Chatwin 72

The New Emperors: Power and the Princelings in China by Kerry Brown
reviewed by Peter Gordon 75

Hard Road Home: Selected Essays by Ye Fu
reviewed by John Butler 78

Exploiting Africa: The Influence of Maoist China in Algeria, Ghana, and Tanzania by Donovan C. Chau
reviewed by Kerry Brown 81

Debating China: The U.S.-China Relationship in Ten Conversations by Nina Hachigian (ed.)
reviewed by Kerry Brown 84

The Chinese Labour Corps: The Forgotten Chinese Labourers of the First World War by Mark O'Neill
reviewed by Juan José Morales 87

The Forbidden Game: Golf and the Chinese Dream by Dan Washburn
reviewed by John D. Van Fleet 90

Asia's Cauldron: The South China Sea and the End of a Stable Pacific by Robert D. Kaplan
reviewed by Peter Gordon 93

Baijiu: The Essential Guide to Chinese Spirits by Derek Sandhaus
reviewed by Jonathan Chatwin 96

Green Politics in China: Environmental Governance and State-Society Relations by Joy Y. Zhang and Michael Barr
reviewed by Coraline Goron 99

China's Second Continent: How a Million Migrants are Building a New Empire in Africa by Howard French
reviewed by Kerry Brown 103

Junkyard Planet: Travels in the Billion-Dollar Trash Trade by Adam Minter
reviewed by Bill Purves 106

Mr. Selden's Map of China: Decoding the Secrets of a Vanished Cartographer by Timothy Brook
reviewed by Tim O'Connell 109

The Virgin Mary and Catholic Identities in Chinese History by Jeremy Clarke
reviewed by Gianni Criveller 113

East Sails West: The Voyage of the Keying, 1846-1855 by Stephen Davies
reviewed by John Butler 118

The Lone Flag: Memoir of the British Consul in Macau during World War II by John Pownall Reeves, edited by Colin Day and Richard Garrett
reviewed by Bill Purves 122

An Anatomy of Chinese: Rhythm, Metaphor, Politics by Perry Link
reviewed by Loh Su Hsing........ 124

Firelight of a Different Colour: The Life and Times of Leslie Cheung Kwok-wing by Nigel Collett
reviewed by Peter Gordon........ 126

Forgotten Voices of Mao's Great Famine, 1958-1962: An Oral History by Zhou Xun
reviewed by Jonathan Chatwin........ 130

Gao Xingjian: Painter of the Soul by Daniel Bergez
reviewed by Loh Su Hsing........ 132

Following the Leader: Ruling China, from Deng Xiaoping to Xi Jinping by David M Lampton
reviewed by Kerry Brown 134

The Siege of Tsingtao by Jonathan Fenby
reviewed by Peter Gordon........ 137

Taming Tibet: Landscape Transformation and the Gift of Chinese Development by Emily T. Yeh
reviewed by Kerry Brown 140

Italy's Encounters with Modern China by Maurizio Marinelli and Giovanni Andornino (eds.)
reviewed by Angelo Paratico........ 143

Lost Generation: The Rustification of Chinese Youth (1968-1980) by Michel Bonnin
reviewed by Kerry Brown 146

At Least We Lived by Emma Oxford; *In Time of War* by Lt. Cmdr. Henry CS Collingwood-Selby
reviewed by Peter Gordon........ 149

Voices from Tibet: Selected Essays and Reportage by Tsering Woeser and Wang Lixiong
reviewed by Kerry Brown 152

Fiction

Black Holes by He Jiahong
reviewed by Peter Gordon 156

From the Old Country: Stories and Sketches of China and Taiwan by Zhong Lihe, edited and translated by TM McClellan
reviewed by John Butler 158

The Unbearable Dreamworld of Champa the Driver by Chan Koonchung
reviewed by John W. W. Zeiser 162

The Ten Thousand Things by John Spurling
reviewed by Jonathan Chatwin 165

I Am China by Guo Xiaolu
reviewed by Loh Su Hsing 167

Night in Shanghai by Nicole Mones
reviewed by Agnès Bun 170

Song of King Gesar by Alai, translated by Howard Goldblatt and Sylvia Li-chun Lin
reviewed by Rosie Milne 174

Children's fiction: *Three Years and Eight Months* by Icy Smith, illustrated by Jennifer Kindert
reviewed by Jane Houng 178

Decoded by Mai Jia
reviewed by Melanie Ho 180

The Ballad of a Small Player by Lawrence Osborne
reviewed by Peter Gordon 183

Mu Shiying: China's Lost Modernist: New Translations and an Appreciation by Andrew David Field
reviewed by John Butler 186

Snow and Shadow by Dorothy Tse, translated by Nicky Harman
reviewed by Peter Gordon 190

Running Through Beijing by Xu Zechen, translated by Eric Abrahamsen
reviewed by Peter Gordon 193

Open Verdict: A Hong Kong Story by Ken Bridgewater
reviewed by Nigel Collett 195

Poetry

Desde Hong Kong: Poets in conversation with Octavio Paz, edited by Germán Muñoz, Tammy Ho Lai-ming and Juan José Morales
reviewed by Henry Wei Leung 200

Something Crosses My Mind by Wang Xiaoni, translated by Eleanor Goodman
reviewed by Jennifer Wong 205

Ancestral Worship: Poems by David McKirdy
reviewed by Agnès Bun 208

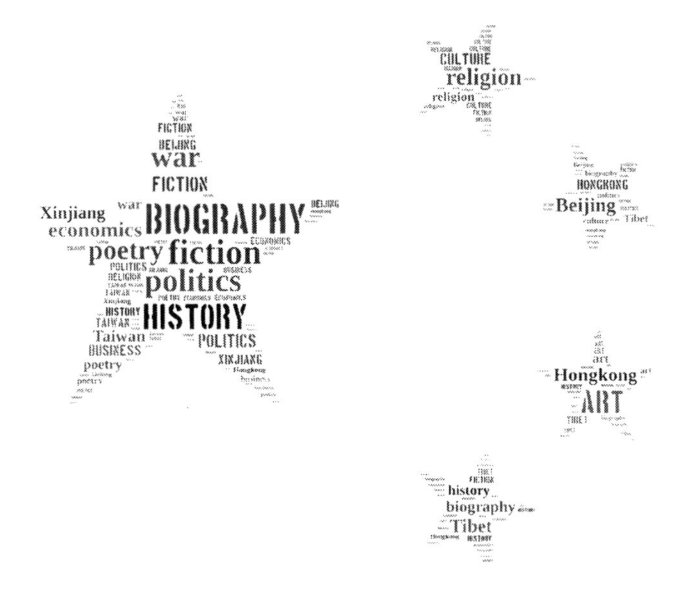
FICTION
BEIJING
war
FICTION
Xinjiang
war
BIOGRAPHY
economics
poetry
fiction
politics
HISTORY
Taiwan
BUSINESS
POLITICS
XINJIANG
poetry
CULTURE
religion
religion
HONGKONG
Beijing
Tibet
Hongkong
ART
history
biography
Tibet

Non-fiction

Meltdown in Tibet: China's Reckless Destruction of Ecosystems from the Highlands of Tibet to the Deltas of Asia by Michael Buckley

reviewed by Sinead Ferris

29 November 2014 — Tibet usually attracts attention because of its unique spiritual heritage and tense political situation; *Meltdown in Tibet* gives us a new reason to worry. Almost every major river in Asia rises on the Tibetan plateau, including the Yangtze, the Mekong, the Irawaddy, the Ganges, and the Indus. More than 750 million people's lives and livelihoods depend directly on these rivers. They are under threat: mining, pollution, damming, diversion and climate change all have the potential to rapidly degrade the quantity and quality of water flowing out of Tibet.

Meltdown in Tibet, by Canadian activist Michael Buckley, uses the construction of hydroelectric dams by Chinese companies in Tibet as a springboard for talking about the social and ecological damage occurring in Tibet.

Hydroelectricity is controversial. Renewable hydro-power is often seen as an essential alternative to China's current dependence on coal-fired power stations. In addition, many people in Tibet's region live without electricity, including nearly 60% of neighboring Nepal. If the power of Tibet's rivers could be harnessed, these people's lives could be significantly improved and their dependence on traditional, carbon-emitting fuel sources reduced. However, dams large enough to provide reliable power have enormous environmental consequences both during and after construction. Huge amounts of carbon are emitted when building the dam, rotting vegetation caught in reservoirs produces the potent greenhouse-gas methane, and large dams severely disrupt river ecosystems.

The social impact can also be brutal, with communities forced to leave their lands and houses to make way for the reservoir. In 2008, more than 1.2 million people were forcibly resettled to make way for the Three Gorges Dam in China's Hubei province. Buckley fears that a similar fate awaits citizens of Tibet.

In the case of Tibet, the humanitarian impact of damming extends far beyond the borders of China. Tibet's rivers support populations in Nepal, Bangladesh, India, Pakistan, Laos, Vietnam and Burma. Rivers from the Tibetan plateau are essential sources of fish and water for crops, and as such are a vital part of each nation's food security mix. Despite great progress, these downstream countries still contain some of the world's most food-insecure people and they are incredibly vulnerable to the effects of altered water flow.

Tibet's strategic location and essential waters mean that degradation of rivers there has important geopolitical consequences. There is a very real danger that the greatest conflicts of this century will be fought over water and food security. Asia is a high risk area, where culturally diverse, fast growing, nationalistic countries must share a diminishing stock of vital resources. The area around Tibet is already contested, claimed by both India and China, and the risk of conflict flaring up over vital water access is a real one.

As if the specter of strategic competition for water between Asia's giants isn't terrifying enough, Tibet's glaciers are also under threat. Glaciers reflect most of the sunlight that hits them; when they vanish they expose the darker ground beneath, which absorbs the sun's heat instead. This further increases the local temperature and causes more melting. Given that Tibet's glaciers comprise the world's third largest store of frozen fresh water, their accelerating melting could have consequences for the entire globe.

The situation is being worsened by the release of "black carbon" from the incomplete burning of fossil fuels in old-style stoves and motors. The minuscule black particles travel thousands of kilometres in air currents from all over the region to settle on Tibet's glaciers. They darken the surface, reducing reflectivity and speeding up dangerous glacier melt. This phenomenon is well documented but not well publicized. According to Buckley, it is also largely avoidable. Efforts have already been made in China to replace old-style cooking stoves and traditional heating methods with cleaner, more efficient technologies—this should be a priority for all of Tibet's regional neighbors, and one developed nations should assist with.

However, not all of the solutions to Tibet's problems are as simple as phasing out old engines, stoves and power plants. The tension between development and poverty reduction on one hand and protection of human rights and the environment on the other is real here, as in any discussion of China. China has a history of overlooking environmental impact in pursuit of economic gains. China is today learning from these past mistakes, but Tibet's rivers are too significant to be another learning experience.

Michael Buckley is extremely passionate about Tibet's political freedom. He set himself up as an authority on travel in the region by writing the first guidebook to Tibet (Lonely Planet 1986), and *Meltdown*, his latest in a long string of publications on the Tibetan plateau, demonstrates clearly that he is angry about the human rights and environmental violations occurring there. This is not a nuanced book—a casual reader could be forgiven for inferring that all Tibetans are saints and all Chinese are monsters—with the unfortunate consequence of probably limiting the readership of *Meltdown* to those who already agree with his opinion of China.

Even more problematically, Buckley's solution to Tibet's looming ecological disaster, one that will wreak havoc on the region, is to call for the political emancipation of Tibet. Although a political solution to an environmental crisis may seem counterintuitive, *Meltdown* argues that, since Tibetan traditional beliefs forbid excessive tampering with nature, if Tibetan religious authorities were still in charge instead of the—in his view—rapacious Han, no environmental damage would be occurring. Even if this is true—and as the black carbon case indicates, the sources of Tibet's environmental problems lie to a certain extent outside its borders—it is unhelpful. Tibet's political situation and its environmental one may both have been caused by China's policies, but that doesn't detract from the fact that they are separate problems with potentially separate solutions. In focusing so heavily on politics, Buckley avoids presenting any realistic resolution of the environmental problem beyond criticizing China. It is unclear whether he would accept improved environmental outcomes in Tibet if unaccompanied by political changes.

This murkiness of argument is unfortunately characteristic of the book. Buckley is a travel writer: his book is short, informal and peppered with personal anecdotes about kayaking trips and yak butter tea. Further, Buckley's overriding annoyance at China leads him to bring in considerations (such as territorial disputes in the South China Sea) that are irrelevant to the matter of Tibet's environmental problems. Many of the issues are complex—not just scientifically, but also socially, economically and politically—and require more than the page or less of explanation that Buckley sometimes affords them. His unwillingness to ever acknowledge that a different perspective might lead to different conclusions weakens rather than strengthens the argument. *Meltdown in Tibet* reads more like an emotional call to arms than anything else.

One of the book's most astute observations is that "water has no border". This is hopefully the idea that shines through: Tibet's rivers must be better managed or the consequence will be an ecological, geopolitical and humanitarian catastrophe.

Meltdown in Tibet: China's Reckless Destruction of Ecosystems from the Highlands of Tibet to the Deltas of Asia, Michael Buckley (Palgrave MacMillan Trade, November 2014)

Chinese Rules: Mao's Dog, Deng's Cat, and Five Timeless Lessons from the Front Lines in China by Tim Clissold

reviewed by Peter Gordon

13 November 2014 — Tim Clissold writes very well, so well in fact that it hardly matters what he writes about. His new book *Chinese Rules*, very much a sequel to the well-received *Mr China* of a decade ago, is conversational in tone, never lingering, never boring.

Clissold comes across as just the sort of fellow you'd want to sit across from on one of those interminable bus rides he, and other foreign businessmen in China, take so many of: a good raconteur who will while away the hours with interesting stories and useful observations. One suspects that Clissold is not without practice in recounting this story.

This time, in 2005—not long after Mr China was published—he's tapped to help clear up a huge carbon credits deal that's gone pear-shaped. Clissold knows nothing about carbon credits, but this doesn't stop him anymore this time than did similar lack of experience in Mr China. So within 24 hours, he's on a plane to China *en route* to Quzhou. When he gets there, he finds a tangle of bureaucracy, face, Chinese government regulations, UN regulations, politics and a London-based financial client who has projected the City onto backcountry China. Clissold concludes, for neither the first nor the last time, that foreigners just don't get it.

He gets stiffed by the client so he and the other key person—an Australian who has been named Mina for the purposes of the book—set off to start their own carbon credits business. This is something of a replay of *Mr China*: huge amounts of money are raised on a phone call, facts are made up and much documentation is false, and deals rely on a single key Chinese person about whom no one knows very much and who is entirely untrustworthy.

Somewhat anti-climactically, they never actually do much business before the market collapses and everything is wound up. But with Clissold, the destination is the journey.

This might make for rather a thin book, so Clissold has also included potted, but readable, chunks of history: Lord Macartney's trip to the Qing Court at the end of the eighteenth century, the Taiping Rebellion, Mao, the Cultural Revolution, Deng. These then lead to Clissold's "five Chinese Rules", which start off with observations like "China is a civilization masquerading as a state" and Chinese people have "an intense dread of instability". Each chapter begins with a proverb or quotation from a Classical chinese text.

Fair enough. It all reads very well. It does however read far better as narrative non-fiction than as the guide to doing business in China that the publishers apparently wish to position it as. Regardless of whether these are indeed "the five key Chinese rules that anyone can deploy on the ground with their [sic] modern Chinese counterparts", as the back cover would have it, anyone who actually has Chinese counterparts might be well-advised to do what Clissold himself actually does: a lot of research, a lot of reading, a lot of observing and a lot of listening.

Chinese Rules, then, is observant, erudite and pleasant. But some deeper issues fall out from between its covers. One of these is the not always salubrious effect that finance has on the real world and on China in particular. There might be some possible benefit in Western firms paying to reduce prospective (not always even actual) carbon emissions in China so they themselves can continue to emit, but it seems hard to come up with an economic or environmental justification for financial firms to make a killing on these transactions.

Clissold writes that this is all in a good cause, reducing global emissions overall and reducing Chinese pollution in particular, but the means to this end require taking more than a few liberties with the truth, principles of transparency and, on occasion, sobriety. At times, it feels like he's trying to convince himself as much as his readers.

Clissold himself never seems terribly concerned with financial return; rather, he seems to treat these projects as puzzles which he feels compelled to understand and solve. Nevertheless, large amounts of money dropping from the Western sky into China for not doing something had the effect one might have predicted. Where there's brass, there's muck, to turn the saying around.

A second and in some ways more fundamental question is whether Chinese business practices—which arguably are different than those in the West—are the result of thousands of years of Chinese history which has somehow burned its way into the Chinese psyche or whether they are instead a rational response to current Chinese conditions. The latter, one would have thought, would have been the default hypothesis.

While it is true, as Clissold remarks, that an "agreement" in China means far less than it does in the City or on Wall Street—that relations, trust and practical conditions are much more important than the actual words on the paper—this can be explained by noting that the Chinese legal system doesn't work very well.

And while Chinese certainly turn to classic texts for guidance and inspiration—Americans at one time turned to *Poor Richard's Almanac*—the Chinese, Clissold himself notes, also turn to Bill Gates. Immigrant Chinese entrepreneurs in the US and Britain, of which there are many, seem perfectly content to rely on contracts, courts, formal finance, and the like. And if there is one thing all shades of Chinese in Hong Kong agree on, it's the importance of the rule of law.

Perhaps business in China is different because China has different operating conditions, not because Chinese are different.

Chinese Rules; Mao's Dog, Deng's Cat, and Five Timeless Lessons from the Front Lines in China, Tim Clissold (HarperCollins Publishers, October 2014)

City of Darkness Revisited by Greg Girard and Ian Lambot

reviewed by Mark L. Clifford

11 November 2014 — When it heaved with life, the Kowloon Walled City was notorious. The enclave, protected by a historical quirk from British rule in Hong Kong, embodied a tangle of fears in the collective consciousness—it was a place of opium and whoredom, lawlessness and murder. It epitomized crime and overcrowding, triads amidst the tenements, chaos in the midst of civilization.

Two decades after its destruction, the Walled City has acquired an increasingly shiny gloss of respectability. Architects of the new urbanism celebrate its dense, human, organic development. The government's dystopian view of the Walled City as a place of "notorious… drug divans, criminal hide-outs, vice dens and even [sic] cheap unlicensed dentists," has given way to a vision of the Walled City in the collective imagination as the lost paradise, a sort of Atlantis, Xanadu and urban Shangri-La rolled into one.

Symbolizing this re-imagined city, and helping make the gloss even shinier, is a new and dramatically expanded twentieth-anniversary edition of *City of Darkness*. In its earlier editions, the book was smoothing of a cult classic. It was also a book that focused very much on the people of the City, trying to de-mystify and humanize this place of urban myth.

The new edition is big and bold, a colorful heavyweight book perfectly suited for gift-giving and coffee-table viewing by people who never would have gone to the City while it was real. But it is also a far more ambitious attempt to look at the underside of the city and at its larger global and urban-architectural dimensions.

The sometimes tight, cramped look of the original has been replaced by larger photos. A number of new essays bring more depth and richness to the book. Fionnula McHugh's essay on the politics of the Walled City clearance sheds light on a secretive chapter in Sino-British relations that until now has remained untold. There is also additional material on the unique architecture and the global influence that the Walled City has come to exercise, especially in the years since it was torn down.

The density of the 14-story Walled City was unequalled anywhere: If Manhattan were built to the same density it would be home not to 1.6 million people but to 65 million. Most informal settlements spread out, but the Walled City was forced to go up, limited to the footprint outlined by the grounds of a former Chinese military compound that was, as the result of a historical quirk, not subject to formal British rule. As recently as the 1960s, pig pens and garden plots had been a feature of the settlement but the city's growth and its hunger for space—space for living, for working, for praying, for eating—saw the City caught up in the race to build Hong Kong. The City only topped out when the government forced the demolition of the top stories of a building that breached the 150' height limit imposed because of the proximity to Kai Tak Airport.

This lavishly-illustrated book centers on Greg Girard's striking photos. But the volume ranges broadly over the past 150 years. A detailed 1865 photo of the old fort, surrounded by hills and rice paddies, and a number of other striking historical photos trace the City's development.

A summary history details the repeated thwarting of British attempts to impose state control on the 0.01 square-mile home to 35,000 people. In pragmatic accommodation to reality, electricity, postal and water service were all provided, despite the lack of formal legal jurisdiction. This was a space that existed in a permanent state of ambiguity and yet had to deal with the reality of two tonnes of garbage a day adds richness to interesting vignettes by, among many others, a postman and a China Light & Power engineer who discuss the daily reality of working in the Walled City.

The Walled City's state of organic anarchism was summed up by author William Gibson:

> [T]here was no law there. An outlaw place. And more and more people crowded in; they built it up, higher. No rules, just building, just people living. Police wouldn't go there. Drugs and whores and gambling. But people living, too. Factories, restaurants. A city."

This is a fascinating, rich book. It is one that can be casually flipped through but it is, above all, a rich and deep work that benefits from repeated reading.

Anyone who loves Hong Kong's grittiness will enjoy this book, for it is all here. The triads and the illegal dentists, the cops and the junkies, the racing-pigeon breeder and the noodle-maker, the mah-jong players and the metal-working factories. As Ian Lambot writes of the original impetus behind the project that he and Greg Girard first conceived of more than 20 years ago:

> [I]n a way, the City stood as a microcosm of Hong Kong—just ordinary people trying to get by in the best way they could.

Few books capture ordinary people in an extraordinary city as richly and lovingly as does *City of Darkness*.

City of Darkness Revisited, Greg Girard, Ian Lambot (Watermark, August 2014)

From the Tsar's Railway to the Red Army: The Experience of Chinese Labourers in Russia during the First World War and Bolshevik Revolution by Mark O'Neill

reviewed by Juan José Morales

9 November 2014 — While several of the Penguin China "specials" have drawn lines between the First World War and the later Communist revolution, most of these lines have passed through Europe, notable France. However, another line passes through Russia. From the *Tsar's Railway to the Red Army* traces the virtually unknown episode of Chinese laborers who went to help Russia's war efforts and who ended being caught up in the maelstrom of the Bolshevik Revolution.

Author Mark O'Neill has already contributed a volume about the Chinese laborers on the Western front (*The Chinese Labour Corps: The Forgotten Chinese Labourers of the First World War*) to which this can be considered a companion. This is still an under-researched area and the true number of Chinese laborers sent to Russia is unknown, but the most likely estimate puts the figure around 200,000 men, more indeed than the 135,000 workers that went to France and Belgium. And they had it far worse, perhaps the most tragic chapter in 400 years of Chinese emigration.

The author begins by sketching the background of the historical relations between the two countries. The Russian empire had greatly expanded east and south during the second half of the nineteenth century to the Amur River and beyond. This was a period of extreme weakness for China, which had to accept the river as the new border; it also allowed Russia to build a port and naval base at Vladivostok. Russia needed and used Chinese labor to develop this area and also to construct railways, including the Far Eastern segment of the Trans-Siberian Railway, and the China Eastern Railway (CER), through the north of Manchuria, via Harbin, to Vladivostok.

Russia's involvement in the War was disastrous from the start, with a devastating number of casualties. China offered a ready supply for the ensuing shortage of workers, and there was a previous experience. However, Beijing lost control of the recruiting. Many workers went to Russia without proper contracts that would have guaranteed basic rights. Poorly equipped and fed, without any protection, the workers were left vulnerable to abuse by middlemen or Russians employers in a web of corruption akin to what today would be termed human trafficking.

Chinese workers began to arrive in Russia in 1916 and were sent all over the Empire. Thousands worked and died at the front. Conditions could be extreme, nowhere more so than in the construction of the railway line from the capital of Petrograd (St Petersburg) to the new ice-free port of Murmansk, on the Kola Peninsula above the Arctic Circle, where many perished due to extreme weather, malnutrition and disease. The 10,000 Chinese who worked here were not alone: they were joined by some 50,000 prisoners of war from the German and Austro-Hungarian armies and 30,000 hired Russian peasants. Chinese workers were also sent to mine coal in the Donets Basin in eastern Ukraine, some of the most hazardous mines in the world. One of the workers, Li Zhen-dong, reflected on their plight:

> We worked in a forest not far from Petrograd. We were seeking a better life but were slaves to hardship. Working in Russia was like working in China. We had to work fifteen hours a day and slept in caves that were humid; they were crowded and dirty. We were paid little, scarcely enough to feed ourselves.

Conditions worsened as the war drew on, for ordinary Russians but more so for the Chinese, who lacked the means to return home, while the Russian employers or Chinese contractors would not repatriate them. The workers were moved to one job to another, and sold, like slaves. Inflation shot up, the shortages of food and fuel became acute, plus the enormous casualties sustained by the Russian army, all led to political upheavals with a society in disarray.

When the Tsarist regime fell and Lenin made a separate peace with

Germany, the Chinese laborers were left stranded in a foreign land. Some were driven to begging or crime, which stigmatized the Chinese community as a whole. To alleviate the situation, some Chinese students, later joined by Chinese diplomats and businesspeople, set up networks of solidarity, such as the Union of Chinese Workers in Russia (UCWR) based in Petrograd. The UCWR found more cooperation with the Soviets than with the Tsarist regime, and developed to become an organisation to reckon with, led by Liu Zerong, a native from Guangzhou, who in March 1919 represented overseas Chinese at the first meeting of the Communist International.

Thousands of Chinese joined the revolution and the Red Army to escape from their miserable situation, or from intimidation, or lured by the promises of a new era for the working class. Prominent among them was Ren Fuchen, considered China's first Bolshevik. Born in 1884 in Liaoning, at fourteen he had started working for a Russian company building the railway from Harbin to Dalian. He joined the Bolsheviks and later became a commander of the Chinese Red Eagle battalion. He was killed in action in November 1918. The book's title summarizes in his personal story those of many Chinese workers.

The Russian Civil War also led to China's involvement on its easternmost border and, eventually, Chinese civilians were evacuated from Vladivostok.

Relations between the Soviet Union and China—paramount for an understanding of modern history—began with these workers. Probably for the first time, the bleak story of the lost contingent of Chinese workers has been brought to light for a larger public.

From the Tsar's Railway to the Red Army: The Experience of Chinese Labourers in Russia during the First World War and Bolshevik Revolution, Mark O'Neill (Penguin China, August 2014)

Living Karma: The Religious Practices of Ouyi Zhixu by Beverley Foulks McGuire

reviewed by John Butler

7 November 2014 —

> My body, mind, and the outer world suddenly disappeared. I then knew that my body came from beginningless time and perishes in the very spot it is born. It is only a shadow manifested by entrenched delusion.

This stunning revelation from his *Autobiography* (included as an appendix) was recorded by the twenty-three year old Ouyi Zhixu (1599-1655), a Chinese Buddhist monk whose belief in the possibility that one could change one's karma is here explained in full for the first time in English by Beverley McGuire, an Assistant Professor of East Asian Studies at the University of North Carolina, who developed this book from her 2009 Harvard dissertation on Ouyi.

As suggested in the marketing for this book, it

> sheds much-needed light on a little-known figure and his representation of karma, which proved to be a seminal innovation in the religious thought of late imperial China...

As McGuire points out, Buddhism in the later part of the Ming Dynasty (it fell in 1644) has been rather neglected by scholars in the field. Furthermore, as a decided non-expert in Buddhist studies, this reviewer can state that in spite of the apparently esoteric nature of the content, McGuire has managed to produce an eminently readable and interesting book which shows us what the inner world of a seventeenth-century Buddhist monk looked like, and how he applied the rituals and practices of his religion to his spiritual (and physical) life.

This is a scholarly book based on a great deal of specialised research, but it's surprisingly accessible to anyone with an interest in Buddhism and its development in China.

Karma is usually understood (at least in part) as a principle of causality, whereby what we do now influences the future outcome of our lives. Many people, Buddhists or otherwise, believe that we cannot escape our karma, and that its consequences are inevitable. The nearest Western term may be "fate" or "destiny", in the sense understood by, say, the Stoics or other philosophers of predetermination.

Definitions and understandings of the term, however, differ; as Professor McGuire notes in her Introduction, "it has expansive connotations that cannot be reduced to cause and effect." This is certainly the case with Ouyi's understanding of it:

> sometimes he suggests that certain religious practices can result in the instant elimination of karma, although at other times he suggests that karmic retribution will still come to fruition.

Ouyi's main contribution to the subject is his assertion that karma is not necessarily inevitable, and that there were things the individual could do to change its course and its effect.

How does Ouyi suggest that we can go about acquiring the power to change our karma? His answer is complex, and involves a great deal of effort on the individual's part. Using himself as an example, Ouyi ranges from simple vows through divination, to repentance and ascetic actions which seem very odd to us at first glance, such as the "filial slicing" of the flesh, the deliberate burning of the arms and head, and even writing Buddhist texts in his own blood, although the ordinary act of writing in pen and ink is still important, indeed an integral part of the process.

If some of these rituals seem strange, readers need only remember that some orders of Christian monks regularly used flagellation, and that some Christians today regularly re-enact the Crucifixion to show their devotion, and that mortification of the flesh is part of some Islamic practices, too.

Repentance, Ouyi suggests, might actually eliminate one's karma altogether, liberating the penitent from the consequences of past actions. Another recommendation from Ouyi is "therapeutic illness"; he wrote in a letter that

> illness is good medicine for our generation. It consumes defilement and deluded thoughts.

Uncannily, in far-off London at about the same time, John Donne, recovering from a serious illness, was writing in his *Devotions upon Emergent Occasions* (1623) that "affliction is a blessing, and no man hath enough of it," and thanking God that his illness had made him meditate more profoundly on what Ouyi calls in his *Autobiography* the "great matter of life and death."

For both men, being ill reinforced the idea that the body is "impermanent and a source of suffering" and that sickness "is an occasion for transforming one's karma," although, of course, Donne would not quite have put it that way. When one is lying in bed experiencing pain and suffering (and the seventeenth century offered few distractions for patients), a heightened sense of awareness may be one of the positive results.

* * *

McGuire divided her book into sections, each one dealing with Ouyi's methods for changing one's karma. Divination is the "karmic diagnostic", followed by repentance "for eliminating karma", vows "to assume the karma of others", and "slicing, burning and blood-writing" to achieve the "karmic transformation of bodies". She discusses each stage of Ouyi's practices in terms of both how they fit into the history of Chinese Buddhism and as texts which invite close reading.

For this reader her most interesting technique for examining Ouyi's thought is the inclusion of the monk's short *Autobiography*, in which he traces his development as a monk from his birth to the age of fifty-three, but he says "my vows were unfulfilled," at which point he dies, and the narrative is taken over by his "unworthy disciple Chengshi", who finishes it for him.

McGuire treats this text (and others) as an act of religious devotion in itself; for her, it is the narrative of religion that matters, and the *Autobiography* provides readers with an insight into the mind of a great religious innovator. If we want to know why he burned his face or wrote in blood, McGuire shows us through her detailed analysis of Ouyi's own writings as they relate to these (to us) bizarre acts and their ethical consequences. She prefers to see the *Autobiography* as having thematic material which can be analysed as having "poetic, instead of referential function," and she refers to "dreams, divination and death" as "tropes" or "imaginative discourse", which show "how a person's connection to sects or groups is more fluid than fixed."

These tropes are more important at the beginning of the *Autobiography* than at the end, where, as McGuire points out,

> they gradually give way to themes of ritual and writing, which fall squarely within the realm of Ouyi's control and responsibility.

The *Autobiography* demonstrates how Ouyi regained, as it were, control over his karma, and was able to suggest in his writings how this could be achieved by others who wished to free themselves from the inexorable.

Ouyi Zhixu was a man who ran against the stream, and as such has been neglected by Buddhist scholars and is hardly known in the West. McGuire not only re-examines his teachings and places them within the history of Chinese Buddhism, but allows us, through the *Autobiography* and her quotations from Ouyi's letters, to get to know something of the mind of this significant and extraordinary man.

Living Karma: The Religious Practices of Ouyi Zhixu, Beverley Foulks McGuire (Columbia University Press, September 2014)

Picnics Prohibited: Diplomacy in a Chaotic China During the First World War by Frances Wood

reviewed by Peter Gordon

3 November 2014 — Had Penguin China published all the various World War One "specials" as a book, one chapter less catching than the others would probably have passed unremarked. But each was published as a stand-alone book, and Frances Wood's *Picnics Prohibited: Diplomacy in a Chaotic China During the First World War* is somewhat drier and doesn't have quite the same number of "oh, I didn't know that" moments of some of the companion volumes.

That being said, it is about diplomacy and diplomacy is not normally (*pace* the odd novel by William Boyd) a subject that gets the blood racing. So maybe the very accomplished historian Wood just pulled the short straw when it came to topics.

The trouble is that not a great deal happened. China tried to get into the War, but the allies weren't keen for a number of reasons: they still wanted the Boxer reparations, they had a low opinion of the Chinese army and they feared the Japanese would wangle the officer positions and end up controlling the Chinese military, although the British Military attaché Lieutenant Colonel Robinson was relatively sanguine on the latter point:

> Japan has yet to show that she is capable of doing with alien races what the Anglo-Saxon has shown can be done in the case of India ...

When America joined, there was no keeping China out.

Not much happened in Shanghai either, but Robert Bickers in his volume *Getting Stuck in For Shanghai* had a deep cast of characters to draw from.

Wood likewise quotes massives of primary sources so we are, as in the other volumes, able to hear the voices of the protagonists. The British seem to have been mostly snobs, the Americans rational but perhaps a bit innocent in expecting others to be as well, and the Italians somewhat dramatic. Count Sforza, the Italian Minister, thought the War would go on for thirty years (although, arguably, he was right). Certain episodes seem Ruritanian: the same Sforza causes a row when his British counterpart, Sir John Jordan, showed up at an "unofficial" dinner with his decorations while Sforza had left his at home. Jordan stripped down to shirtsleeves and removed his marks of distinction.

The diplomatic corps had its hands full entertaining (since the belligerents wouldn't sit at the same table with each other, the neutral countries had to hold each dinner party twice), ignoring overly-enthusiastic reports of sightings of German spies and being conned by Edward Trelawney Backhouse, who claimed to be able to source hundreds of thousands of Western-manufactured guns in China for the Allied war effort.

The main concern, however, was Japan, which was all too clearly on the make. But the other Allies usually let the Japanese get away with whatever they were up to, including at the Peace Conference in Paris; that turned out quite badly indeed.

So while the diplomatic to-ings and fro-ings don't have quite the dash of the siege of Tientsin, the earthiness of some of the characters along the Shanghai Bund or the panache of the Chinese delegation to Paris, Wood fills a crucial gap with *Picnics Prohibited* and brings to life a cast of characters less prominent in the other volumes in the series.

She also describes a world and Downton Abbey-ish world-view on which the clock was running out very quickly, not that the participants seem to have realized it.

Picnics Prohibited: Diplomacy in a Chaotic China During the First World War, Frances Wood (Penguin China, August 2014)

Chinese Comfort Women: Testimonies from Imperial Japan's Sex Slaves by Peipei Qiu, with Su Zhiliang and Chen Lifei

reviewed by Jonathan Chatwin

19 October 2014 — That Japanese soldiers were responsible for widespread sexual violence during the second Sino-Japanese war is well-known. Immediately following the end of the war, Chiang Kai-Shek established tribunals to investigate the atrocities committed by the Japanese Army; continuing under Communist rule, these made known the scale of the mistreatment of Chinese civilians and soldiers.

Contemporary Chinese sentiment towards Japan continues to be strongly influenced by the stories of brutality which emerged, and which have become part of a cultivated national narrative. Outside of China, Iris Chang's bestselling *The Rape of Nanking* (1997) brought the atrocities committed in that city to popular attention in the West.

However, though the overall narrative is now well-known, the stories told in *Chinese Comfort Women* reveal new horrors. The volume details, for the first time in English, the traumatic experiences of the women known in Japanese as *ianfu*—a euphemism generally translated as "comfort women". These women were abducted or lured by the Japanese troops, and forced into lives of sexual slavery. Though the "comfort stations" where the women were held to service Japanese soldiers differed in scale and organisation, the experiences of those held are uniformly harrowing.

The book is built around the personal narratives of twelve survivors of the comfort stations—most of whom had died or were seriously ill by the time of the book's publication. These are gruelling first-hand accounts, both of the women's wartime abuse and the subsequent hardships and prejudice they endured after the end of the war. Bookending these narratives are chapters providing historical context, both as to the events of the war itself, and the legal campaign for redress that continues to be pursued, and with which the authors are closely involved.

The lives of the women interviewed in *Chinese Comfort Women* were shattered by their wartime experiences. Having had to endure repeated sexual violence, all suffered from severe health problems for the remainder of their lives. Many were rendered infertile by the brutality. After release, they were often shunned by their communities. Lu Xiuzhen was kept as a comfort woman on Chongming Island:

> Because I had been raped by the enemy, people in my village gossiped about me, saying that I slept with Japanese soldiers. I was unable to find a prospective husband until I was thirty-three years old [...] People in my village believed that a person defiled by Japanese soldiers would bring bad luck and could not produce anything good. They said I could not even grow things well in the fields.

* * *

Chinese Comfort Women is a fundamentally political book. It aims to advance the ongoing legal action against Japan, in which redress is sought for the sufferings of those affected by the comfort women system. As such it is a polemic—but such is the tragedy of the women's experience that one overlooks any partisanship. It is also rigorous—scrupulously researched and demonstrating the highest academic integrity.

Japan has been accused of running down the clock on the issue of compensating Chinese comfort women; the reality is that the already small number of survivors who remain to be compensated is reducing with each year that passes. Their cause has not been helped by the attitude of the Chinese authorities, for whom the campaign seems a source of embarrassment; the authors tell the story of one survivor, Li Lianchun, who was refused the travel documents necessary for her to attend the Women's International War Crimes Tribunal because a local official felt that it was "inappropriate for her to speak of her 'shameful past' abroad."

The campaign will continue nonetheless. As Li, who died before the publication of the book, explained:

> The damage done to [my body] cannot be compensated for with money, no

matter how much money they pay. I am not seeking money, and I am not trying to get revenge. I just want to see justice done.

Chinese Comfort Women: Testimonies from Imperial Japan's Sex Slaves, Peipei Qiu, Su Zhiliang, Chen Lifei (Hong Kong University Press, July 2014; Oxford University Press USA, June 2014; University of British Columbia Press, November 2013)

Villages in the City: South China's Informal Settlements and *Factory Towns of South China*, edited by Stefan Al; *Paris Reborn* by Stephane Kirkland

reviewed by Mark L. Clifford

8 October 2014 — The city was one vast construction zone. New streets were literally smashed through buildings. Half-demolished buildings dominated the cityscape. Roads were ripped apart and mountains of rubble piled up.

> It is a curious spectacle to see these open houses with their colored or flowered wallpaper still showing the shapes of bedrooms, their stairs that no longer lead anywhere, their strange declivities and their violent ruins.

This was mid-nineteenth century Paris—in a description quoted by Stephane Kirkland—as the city was reshaped to realize the grand vision of Emperor Napoleon III. Between 1852 and 1870, 27,000 buildings were knocked down. Some 350,000 people, more than 20 percent of the population, were forced to move.

Napoleon III is one of the only emperors we know who had a giant map of his capital city in his study. Part work scheme, part morality play, part hygiene-driven urban renewal, Napoleon III's vision to transform Paris was famously carried out by Georges-Eugène Haussmann. After his appointment by the Emperor, Hausmann quickly set about, in his own words

> ripping open the neighborhoods of the center of the city with... their crowded, sordid and unhealthy houses; these neighborhoods that are for the most part a seat of misery and disease and a subject of shame for a great country such as France.

* * *

Much of this will sound familiar to anyone living in China today. In the eyes of the Chinese media, a village that stands in the way of lucrative high-rise property development is derided as an "eyesore", "cancer", an "ill" that is a "scar" on the city. The residents of these poorer areas are labelled as filthy, as burglars, drug users and even murders.

As in Second Empire Paris, so too in China today: governments exercise their power of eminent domain to seize land. It is a contest, naturally, with the state and its development allies against those who stand to lose their apartments. Importantly, it is also a struggle between the state and private developers over profits. For urban real estate redevelopment can be spectacularly lucrative, whether in Paris or Shenzhen. Money, as much as vision, drives urban change.

Few other cities could rival Paris by the time the Second Empire drew to an end. Victor Hugo, the curmudgeonly opponent to Haussmann's vision, proclaimed a new era for a more united Europe at the time of the 1867 Paris Exposition. "Before having its people, Europe has its capital." Paris had become, in Kirkland's words, "hands down the most glamorous and exciting place in the world." This urban architectural unity was bought at a terrible cost, the price of the Second Empire's corrupt, rapacious, excessive, sensual but, in the end, successful modernization project, one with a violent ending. Napoleon III's defeat at the hands of Prussia and the dissolution of the Second Empire set in motion a chain of events that saw some 10,000 people killed during the Bloody Week that marked the crushing of the Paris Commune in May 1871.

Napoleon III's modernization project was one that his Republican opponents carried on after the end of the Second Empire. The boulevard

Saint-Germain and the avenue de l'Opéra were completed soon after the war with Prussia ended. The same length of streets were built in the two decades following 1870 as during the 18 years of the Second Empire. The construction of the Metro, the Universal Expositions and the building out of the city's infrastructure, all continued after Republicans took power. "We only wish one thing today," said deputy Jules Simon shortly after the Third Republic was declared in 1870, "that we complete through liberty what was started by despotism."

Paris today is a city frozen in time. The Notre-Dame's current incarnation is a Haussmann-era reconstruction, and not a particularly historically accurate one. The iconic *bateaux-mouches* that ply the Seine and the grand boulevards would be recognizable to people from Napoleon III's time. The Eiffel Tower of two decades later and IM Pei's 1989 Louvre pyramid are virtually the only significant architectural additions to the center of the city. The challenge of Paris is to leave the nineteenth century a little further behind and to adapt to the twenty-first century.

China's conundrum today is akin to that of Second Empire Paris: the challenge of managing growth and modernization. What is happening in China, indeed throughout Asia and the developing world, is urbanization on a scale that the world has never witnessed. In China alone, almost 20 million people a year are becoming urban dwellers. What was a country of peasants when Deng Xiaoping began his economic reforms in 1978 is now made up mostly of city dwellers.

The scale of this city-building has no precedent. The Pearl River Delta, that megalopolis stretching from Hong Kong up the eastern side of the delta to Guangzhou and back down the western side to Macau is home to something on the order of 70 million people. Consider that Napoleon III's Paris had fewer than 2 million people—and that all of France today has a population about the same as the Delta.

How do we make sense of China's urbanization, given its scale and its seeming chaos? Architect and professor Stefan Al has come out with two volumes that help sort out Southern China's project of modernization and development, both its factory complexes and its urban villages. Both works go inside the areas they study, and are generously illustrated with photographs, drawings and maps.

Villages in the City, the more recent of the two volumes and a companion to *Factory Towns of South China*, documents the peculiar phenomenon of what are nominally farming villages now surrounded by high-rises. For migrants from other parts of China these villages are a place for low-cost housing. They have many of the qualities celebrated by new urbanists—the villages are dense and, because many of these are illegally built structures, do not have elevators and are by necessity fairly low-rise. The streets are extremely narrow, enforcing pedestrianization.

The farmer-owners who build the "handshake houses"—narrow enough to reach out to touch a neighbor across the way—have profited. Unlike the buildings of medieval Paris whose destruction by Haussmann was lamented by Victor Hugo and others, there is little architectural merit in these cheaply built concrete buildings covered with cheap ceramic tiles. Certainly, they are an affront to the planners and developers who want to see them give way to the high-rise towers that make up Chinese cities.

These settlements live in limbo, enjoying a measure of legal protection thanks to their status as agricultural villages, owned by rural collectives. As the high-rises have literally dwarfed these low-rise settlements, city officials and developers have tried to convert them to urban areas. In 2000, the Guangzhou government set a goal of wiping out the 138 remaining villages in the city's central districts by 2015.

* * *

How China completes its urbanization project, which has more than another decade to run as rural immigrants continue to be absorbed, is uncertain. On the positive side, China has done a superb job building infrastructure, from power plants to roads. Unfortunately, this infrastructure is far too focused on automobiles and too little on other modes of transport.

China excels in the neo-Brutalism of large public spaces and overawing buildings, designed to impress, but leaving little space for people, especially for pedestrians—and virtually none for bicycles. There are the large boulevards and the impressive network of ring roads, yet traffic is in a state of semi-permanent gridlock. Vast complexes combine high-rise apartments, shopping malls and, often, office spaces, but they are cut off from one another, like an archipelago. There is none of the urban coherence of

Paris or New York, none of the serendipity of Tokyo or London.

Paris is a city where one could be deposited blindfolded and instantly know that one was in Paris. In China, the stifling uniformity means that one would only know that he was somewhere in China. Most damningly, China is not building sustainable cities for its future. China's impressive infrastructure notwithstanding, its buildings squander energy. Although it is three to four times cheaper to build energy-efficient buildings in China than it is to build the coal-fired power plants to heat, cool and light these buildings, the country continues to build remarkably inefficient buildings. It has laws to promote energy efficiency, but lacks the grassroots network of citizen involvement and civil society to make energy-efficient buildings a success.

Although China is building on a far larger scale, and with much less of the beauty, than Haussmann's Paris, the methods have an eerie similarity. Perhaps China is not as different as many observers, and the Chinese themselves, often believe.

Urban development in China, as with so many of the changes taking place, are perceived by those in the middle of the change as somehow having no precedent, of standing outside of history. History doesn't repeat itself, but it does rhyme, and Second Empire France is one of those rhymes that China's planners and policy makers would do well to study.

Paris Reborn: Napoleon III, Baron Haussmann, and the Quest to Build a Modern City, Stephane Kirkland (St. Martin's Press, April 2013); *Villages in The City*, Stefan Al (ed.) (Hong Kong University Press, August 2014); *Factory Towns of South China: An Illustrated Guidebook*, Stefan Al (Hong Kong University Press, May 2012)

The South China Sea by Bill Hayton and *Fire on the Water: China, America, and the Future of the Pacific* by Robert Haddick

reviewed by Peter Gordon

5 October 2014 — Bill Hayton's *The South China Sea* opens with a dramatic and alarming scenario of a global conflagration that starts with a pair of Philippine fishing boats sailing out to a shoal in the South China Sea and ends with someone in Delhi deciding that "this would be the perfect moment to regain some lost territory in the Himalayas..." Just in case the historical parallels aren't immediately obvious, he rhetorically asks a paragraph later "What happens if someone shoots an Archduke?"

Our attention secured, the rest of the book is markedly less sensational. Hayton, a longtime BBC reporter, patiently walks us through the South China Sea's many conundrums. He starts with history, indeed prehistory. The purpose of these chapters is to debunk Chinese claims that the South China Sea is "historically" China's. It was not until the 10th century under the Song, for example, that

> After more than one thousand years of trading with foreigners, the people whom we would now call 'Chinese' set sail across the oceans on their own vessels for the first time.

Even then, China hardly dominated.

Archaeology has been made the handmaiden of politics and Hayton dismisses Chinese claims curtly:

> The presence of pottery on any shoal is no more proof of Chinese histori-

> cal possession than the presence of cowry shells in a Bronze Age tomb in the Chinese city of Anyang is proof that Henan Province should rightfully belong to the Philippines.

He notes that 19th-century Chinese writers just translated English or French names for the various rocks, shoals and islands that China now claims centuries-long knowledge of.

Hayton makes a good case that the historical arguments—whether from China or the other claimants—for sovereignty over the South China Sea are less than convincing. Arguments based around international law fare little better:

> Unfortunately, in the South China Sea the law is far from clear. There are two sets of law to contend with: an older form governs 'historical claims' to a territory and a newer form, defined by United Nations Convention on the Law of the Sea (UNCLOS), governs the maritime claims that can be measured from territorial claims. The South China Sea is where the two forms intersect—and perhaps collide.

In the process, *The South China Sea* gives a good overview of a couple millennia of maritime and trade history as well as—no mean task—explaining UNCLOS itself clearly and succinctly. The book is worth reading for this alone.

But the validity of the arguments based on history or international law isn't, nor surely ever was, quite the point. Hayton provides an alternate and better perspective with which to frame the South China Sea dispute: the adoption (or imposition) of the European nation-state system in which "a political unit had become defined by its edges" on the Southeast Asian mandala system where "the ruler's authority diminished with the distance from the centre of the kingdom."

> In the Asian system there could gradual transitions in authority and even gaps where no ruler was acknowledged. Smaller units might recognise more than one sovereign or possibly none at all... In the European system there were no gaps—everywhere was supposed to belong to a sovereign—and to only one.

A zero-sum game in other words, which has manifested itself in the now infamous "nine-dashed line", and one in which China's growing power is an increasingly decisive factor.

* * *

Robert Haddick is a military analyst in Washington and while he doesn't quite have Hayton's flowing, journalistically-honed prose, his new book *Fire on the Water* from the Naval Institute Press—targeted, it is safe to assume, at specialists and policy-makers—is remarkably readable. He also eschews the travelogue-ish anecdotes and detours of Hayton's book which have unfortunately come to seem *de rigueur* in current affairs books for a general audience.

Notwithstanding Haddick's in-depth discussion of weapon systems and strategy—all of which is quite impressive; if military affairs are understood in as much detail as this book suggests, why have the last few American military ventures gone so wrong?—it is the description of China's "salami-slicing" tactics that stands out:

> the slow accumulation of small changes, none of which in isolation amounts to a casus belli, but which can add up over time to a significant strategic change. China's application of steady pressure and increasingly persistent presence on and around disputed claims in the Near Seas is evidence of salami slicing at work.

This tactic itself has probably been apparent to observers, specialist or otherwise, but it helps to be able to give it such an apt and descriptive name.

Nor can the South China Sea be considered as a purely practical matter. What has "China as a whole gained?" asks Hayton.

> The best that can be said is the occupations prevented other countries advancing their positions. No-one else has been able to drill for oil or monopolise fishing activity in the region but despite all the effort that has gone into seizing and building bases, neither has China.

Hayton is skeptical that much in the way of recoverable oil and gas lies beneath the South China Sea; Haddick, who takes a wider geographical remit than just the South China Sea, is more convinced of the potential. But both writers argue that China's position on the various territorial disputes is not based primarily on the potential resource wealth that lies in or beneath the ocean. Indeed, remarks Haddick,

> If... China's main interest in the Near Seas was the exploitation of their vast hydrocarbon potential... it would seem a straightforward matter to set aside sovereignty questions and instead negotiate deals with Japan, Taiwan, Vietnam, the Philippines, and others to develop and share the seas' oil and gas.

He further points out that China has

> settled eleven land border disputes with six of its Northern and Western neighbors since 1998—in many cases ceding more than half of its original claims ... China is thus not opposed on principle to settling territorial claims...

... just not, however, maritime claims.

Both writers conclude that what is really at issue is security, and express not inconsiderable understanding for China's stated and probable concerns.

Hayton finds many if not most Chinese actions and statements to be cynical, but is not dismissive of the underlying issues. The longer second portion of *The South China Sea* details more recent developments as well as the issues of nationalism and military security that bedevil attempts to move any discussion forward. These last few years of the story will be familiar to those who read the papers; *The South China Sea* provides a good *aide-memoire*.

Haddick goes through these incidents and the consequent concerns for the United States's policy-makers in even more considerable and even-handed detail, never downplaying China's security concerns: *Fire on the Water* is a very useful companion volume to the more journalistic *The South China Sea*.

Hayton ends optimistically

> I offer a Mediterranean analogy... It's a semi-enclosed Sea with a shared history and a connected present whose whole is greater than the sum of its parts. It will be a Sea with agreed boundaries based upon universal principles and governed by shared responsibilities to use its resources wisely, a Sea where fish stocks are managed collectively for the benefit of all, where the impacts of oil exploration and international shipping are alleviated and where search and rescue operations can take place unimpeded. It could happen ...

somewhat hoping against hope, one feels.

For Haddick, the United States remains key to regional stability; not that American presence is perfect, but that the alternative would be worse. This must however be a two-way street in ways it has not been in the past. America and its partners, he writes must

> treat China with respect and ensure that China has a clear path for continued success, a path that does not detract from the potential of its neighbors...

Something other than a zero-sum game, therefore. Obvious, perhaps, but far from easy to pull off. Anyone who starts asking "Why can't they just..." should be read either or both of these books to understand that there is no "just" about it.

South China Sea: The Struggle for Power in Asia, Bill Hayton (Yale University Press, October 2014); *Fire on the Water: China, America, and the Future of the Pacific*, Robert Haddick (US Naval Institute Press, September 2014)

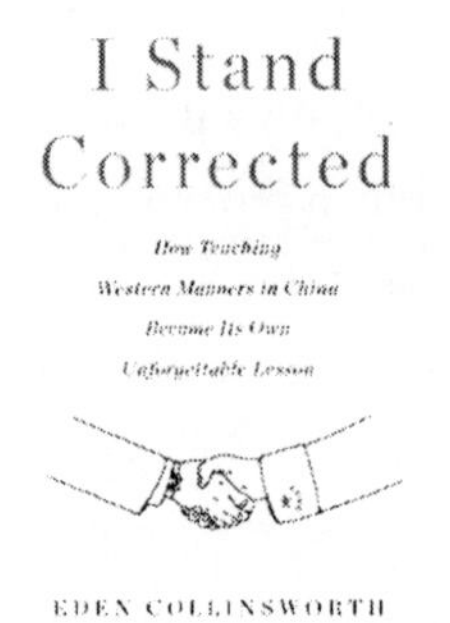

I Stand Corrected: How Teaching Western Manners in China Became Its Own Unforgettable Lesson by Eden Collinsworth

reviewed by Melanie Ho

23 September 2014 — Three years ago, in 2011, Eden Collinsworth moved to Beijing to write *The Tao of Improving Your Likeability: A Personal Guide to Effective Business Etiquette in Today's Global World*, which went on to become a best-seller in China. From the experience writing *Tao* comes Collinsworth's latest effort *I Stand Corrected: How Teaching Western Manners in China Became Its Own Unforgettable Lesson*, a sort of travelogue and memoir that spans not only her year in China, but her career and the years she spent raising her son.

The idea for starting a Western etiquette programme in China stemmed from Collinsworth's Mandarin-speaking son, Gilliam. Collinsworth, who has visited China since the 1980s, sets the plan in motion, thinking that a book would help "build a platform of brand recognition". The former director of cross-media business development at Hearst Corporation, Collinsworth abruptly quits her job as chief of staff for a global think tank and moves to Beijing during her son's university summer break.

From Collinsworth's arrival in Beijing, the reader knows it's going to be a good story. As she registers with the police (Gilliam alongside to translate) she sees that there's no option for a three-month stay. Her son tells her to check off a year.

> "But I'll be doing something illegal if I check the one-year box," I insisted.
>
> "Mother, trust me on this. Everything is slightly illegal in China. That's the point."

Mimicking the organization of an etiquette book, *I Stand Corrected* has sections ranging from introductions and greetings and the art of conversation to censorship and gender politics. Interspersed through the book are various lessons that were included in *Tao* (Lesson 12 instructs one on how to converse with someone you've just met; Lesson 21 deals with appropriate office attire), with reflections on her experiences in China or tales from other travels that inspired said lessons. Woven through the chapters are broader thoughts on how to do business in China, although Collinsworth's fluid style and treasure trove of anecdotes means that she can explain *guanxi* with a story about letter-writing to Angelina Jolie.

While Collinsworth touches on many of the familiar themes of a China memoir, her way of illuminating her personal experiences makes similarities feel fresh. For those who have worked in China, there's an added bonus of feeling like you're speaking with an old friend; there's a sense of "I've been there too." Take, for example, when Collinsworth describes a banquet where the Chinese host began conversing with the woman to his left:

> "I see you like food," was how he began.
>
> "Well, yes, I suppose I do like food," responded the woman, charmed by what she assumed was his limited English.
>
> "I knew that because you are fat," was what he said next.

Those familiar with China can counter with all-too-similar tales of directness (Here's mine: a journalist once asked me my shoe size. I told her and she replied confidently, "Yes, your feet are very big because you didn't wear socks as a child." Just this past weekend I was informed, after exchanging pleasantries, by various Mainland Chinese that my skin was either too dark or not tanned enough.) It's comforting to hear others' experiences—or at least remind myself that I haven't been called fat or old. Yet.

Collinsworth's China experiences may be familiar tales to some, but that doesn't make them any less amusing or worth reading. For those who haven't had the pleasure of doing business in China, the book is a primer for what to expect and advanced warning on the appropriate responses and reactions. Collinsworth works with a client who has spent billions on an empty resort, has a run-in with censors and experiences several Chinese banquet dinners, including one where Mr Han, dissatisfied with the slow pace she took in drinking her Château Lafite Rothschild, showed her the label. Her fellow diners gulped theirs and the bottle was finished in 10 minutes.

China is the obvious focus of the memoir, but Collinsworth weaves in her experiences from all over the world—New York and Los Angeles both make appearances, as does France, Tanzania and Rwanda—and from various points in her life. She speaks of tracking gorillas with her brother in Africa, of rescuing turtles from New York's Chinatown that would have otherwise been made into turtle soup, and of her son's marvelous childhood with adventures that ranged from weekend trips abroad to attending the Lycée Français in Los Angeles (neither parent is French, but W., as the ex is referred to, when suggesting that they not tell their first-grader that he was going to a school where no English was spoken, replied: "The boy doesn't know what school is. He's never been, so how would he know what happens there?"). An explanation of *shengnu*, China's leftover women, is preceded by Collinsworth's own mother saying, "Do you realize how difficult you're becoming to marry off?" after Collinsworth returned from Africa having developed pleurisy.

And while *Tao* was written in Chinese and for a Chinese audience, Collinsworth doesn't pretend that the West has it all together. In Lesson 4, she advises the basics of personal hygiene followed by a note that "anything that requires clipping should be done in the bathroom, preferably yours." But the inspiration for that lesson came not from her experience in China, but from a New York City subway where a man's toenail clippings landed in her lap and another unfortunate encounter in the Cathay Pacific lounge at Hong Kong's airport.

Collinsworth explains Chinese practices in a way that helps reflect on the West's own customs. She touches on subjects from the economy and politics to corruption and the education system as effectively as she does in relaying her own experiences. The book makes it obvious that Collinsworth is, in her words, "forever and beguilingly mystified by the Middle Kingdom."

I Stand Corrected is a funny, self-effacing and quick read—one might consider picking this up ahead of the next flight to Wuhan.

I Stand Corrected: How Teaching Western Manners in China Became Its Own Unforgettable Lesson, Eden Collinsworth (Nan A. Talese, October 2014)

Strangers Across the Border: Indian Encounters in Boomtown China by Reshma Patil

reviewed by Nicholas Gordon

14 September 2014 — Few things seem to cut off communication more than the virtual line that separates two countries; never more so, perhaps, than in the relationship between India and China, arguably the two most important countries in Asia. Despite their close proximity, or perhaps due to it, the two countries' relations can be described as strained at best, rarely progressing past mere cross-border trade. Investment, while growing, is still much lower than the size of their economies would suggest it ought to be. Both countries tend to follow their respective goals alone, despite several areas of potential cooperation (such as climate change and intellectual property).

Strangers Across the Border by Reshma Patil, is motivated by this division. The book is less an in-depth analysis of the China-India relationship than a recollection of Patil's time in China as a reporter for the *Hindustan Times*: one of a very small contingent of Indian reporters in China. This is primarily a book about China and Chinese attitudes (as opposed to one examining Indian attitudes to China), as Patil recounts her meetings with several Chinese and China-based Indians.

The picture Patil paints is one of ignorance. The various people she meets repeat several misconceptions about India, such as the belief that India is a majority-Buddhist nation; at worst, they blatantly parrot racist stereotypes to her face. Several Chinese officials openly express despair that India does not work with China on challenging the West (though they won't go as far as to change policy to accommodate New Delhi's concerns); they simultaneously harangue Patil and other reporters for only writing "negative" stories about Chinese and India (ignoring virulent anti-

India editorials in State-run papers).

Ultimately, Patil argues that China's relatively greater development has led it to ignore India. To the Chinese, China's economic success vindicates both its policy and its place in the world; India, in contrast, is perceived as having pretensions of grandeur and wrongly trying to "punch above its weight". India is often viewed in China as an economic and political model to avoid: Patil notes that several Chinese officials used India as an example of democracy's negative effects.

These are anecdotes filtered through Patil's own perceptions, and so one should be wary of putting too much weight on them. Chinese commentators aren't wrong when they note India's struggles with development and sanitation. The criticisms Patil hears on caste discrimination are likely expressed inaccurately and inartfully, but the comments aren't necessarily entirely wrong; expats—of which I am one—know what its like to react strongly to exaggerated, though not necessarily baseless, criticism of one's country.

However, *Strangers*'s overall point—that Beijing has little interest in New Delhi—still stands. Nor is there much of a grassroots constituency amongst the Chinese public pushing for closer ties with India.

China's view of itself is, unfortunately, not conducive to viewing India as a model or equal partner. China may readily consider India as a supplier of products and services, but not so much as a supplier of ideas. *Strangers* portrays a China that is increasingly self-assured and confident. This China accepts that Japan, Europe and the United States are "equals" to be taken seriously, although this is a fact some Chinese admit only grudgingly. China largely does not think the same of India, whose growth rates have lagged several points behind China. India has, by objective measures, enjoyed less development than China, so why should Beijing listen to it?

This is not a problem unique to this relationship: large countries don't seem to pay much attention to smaller or "less successful" countries. The United States doesn't make much of an attempt to understand anyone; China only seems to take notice of Washington, Tokyo and Berlin. India is not blameless here either; until quite recently, India neglected its immediate neighbors (Pakistan being the significant exception), and it still remains to be seen if this recent interest will hold.

The issue here is that while China should consider India as an equal, it does not and probably won't at least until India shows Chinese levels of growth and development. Thus, the Indian hope that China will suddenly come around to viewing India as a partner as the result of current trends, or by merely talking about trade and investment, is probably misguided.

It's not clear how one solves this. One straightforward solution proposed by Patil is to send more Indians to China. She notes that she is one of a tiny contingent of Indian reporters, and almost no Indian students go to China. She specifically supports sending more Indian CEOs to China, and to more seriously treat China as a potential market for Indian products and investment. This would serve to remove some of the stereotypes around India, such as the idea that the county is "only" good for software and programming.

However, while business contacts help, CEOs will always be focused on how to best increase their company's revenues: a path that may or may not always include China. Essentially, for the long-term presence that would most help, there need to be a lot more Indians that speak Chinese. The inverse—more Chinese speaking English—will not necessarily help, as those Chinese probably have other priorities for their English than India.

Strangers Across the Border, in other words, would indicate that India cannot reasonably expect China to take it seriously unless India makes an more of an initial effort.

Strangers Across the Border, Reshma Patil (HarperCollins India, March 2014)

Chomping at the Bitcoin: The Past, Present and Future of Bitcoin in China by Zennon Kapron

reviewed by Peter Gordon

10 September 2014 — Bitcoin may be the news topic of the past year with the lowest ratio of understanding to awareness. It was perhaps inevitable, therefore, that Bitcoin should have also become the target of rampant speculation in China. This is the subject of the punningly-entitled *Chomping at the Bitcoin*, a Penguin China "Special" by Zennon Kapron.

Bitcoin, for those who somehow managed to remain unaware of it, is a "virtual currency": it doesn't exist in physical form. Nor is backed by anything at all: there is no government, no gold, no reserves in a bank somewhere, nothing.

Kapron finds this almost breathlessly fascinating. But he's right, for Bitcoin is an economics experiment taking place right in front of our eyes. A currency is a currency if people accept it as such and not if they don't: that, in the end, is the only real difference between the dollar and some other national currencies it would be impolite to mention.

And people, some people anyway, do accept Bitcoin. There are two main reasons why. The interesting reason is that the mysterious and as-yet-unidentified inventor solved the problem of preventing copying. This is not an easy problem, for a Bitcoin is just bits, as are MP3s, which are copied all the time. As a corollary of this solution, Bitcoin is distributed throughout the Internet: the "central bank" is in effect the Internet itself. A further corollary is the (according to Kapron, somewhat erroneous) view that Bitcoin is untraceable and is therefore a medium of choice for illicit online dealings.

The second, and less sensible reason, is that the total number of Bitcoins that can ever be in circulation has been limited. With a strictly limited money supply, Bitcoins ought not be subject to inflation. It has been argued that this makes Bitcoin more reliable that so-called national "fiat" currencies which can be manipulated by governments. If this sounds not unlike the arguments made for gold, then it should come as no surprise that the technical activities used to create new Bitcoins are known as "mining".

Kapron goes through the arguments, concisely and as cogently as possible—some of the issues are subtle—as well as looking at other digital currencies that have popped up. Kapron is more sanguine than I that Bitcoin ever was or ever could be a "currency". Because the amount in circulation is capped, Bitcoin is inherently deflationary: goods priced in Bitcoin will get cheaper. (This is the flipside of Bitcoin appreciation.) One's money will buy more tomorrow, so best wait. A currency isn't much good if people are loathe to part with it.

When the value of Bitcoin rocketed in 2013, very much due to speculative demand from China, it looked, and still looks, a lot like a tulip bubble. Kapron recognizes all this but argues there was—and perhaps still is—a possibility that Bitcoin will at some point be accepted as a proper currency, in which case those would bought in early would win the "lottery", as he puts it.

Much and probably all of this has been written about elsewhere and perhaps just as cogently too. But the additional and equally fascinating aspect of the Kapron's little book—at under 90 pages, it is almost more a long-form essay—is China's role in the Bitcoin saga. China has jumped on other bandwagons and ridden them to domestic and global success—Alibaba's upcoming IPO comes to mind—but it hard to think of an example where China has driven the development of a market so quickly and so hard.

Bitcoin's popularity and the investment made in the fundamentally economically useless computer power for "mining" says something both about China as well as its increasing ability to drive global events in business, technology and finance. Although the Chinese government stepped in to regulate Bitcoin, there is no mistaking, says Kapron with some hyperbole, that "it has already had a major impact on every aspect of Chinese society."

Kapron also argues, reasonably convincingly, that sooner or later, a virtual currency—if not necessarily Bitcoin—will catch on, but this requires "the world's second-largest economy as part of the mix." These days, of course, that could be said about just about anything. Will it be possible to roll out the next disruptive technology, the next Google or smartphone, without taking China into account right from the start?

Chomping at the Bitcoin: The Past, Present and Future of Bitcoin in China, Zennon Kapron (Penguin China, August 2014)

By All Means Necessary: How China's Resource Quest is Changing the World by Elizabeth C. Economy and Michael Levi

reviewed by Loh Su Hsing

5 September 2014 — The quest for resources is an excellent angle from which to examine China's rise. This quest encompasses almost all the key issues surrounding the impact of China's resurgence on the rest of the world, from international security to environmental deterioration and corporate social responsibility.

Economy and Levi have put forth an informed, nuanced and balanced analysis of the many facets of China's eager acquisition of natural gas, ores and other resources, along the way offering much-needed clarity and objectivity beyond the simplicity and hype all too often found in the media and newspaper headlines.

The authors open with history. While past growth trajectories do not necessarily reflect future trends, the authors cite the example of postwar Japan, an erstwhile rising economic power which had stoked unfounded fears, suggesting that China could well prove similar. While it could be counter-argued that the vast differences between Japan and China in terms of size, political system, stage of economic development, capacity to adopt technology and perhaps most importantly, Japan's reliance on American military protection render the two not entirely comparable, it is still a sober check to the generally alarmist perspectives on the subject.

Most notably, the authors examine both sides of the equation: how the world has been changed by China's quest for resources and how China itself has in turn been molded from exposure to global norms and practices through its trade and investments.

By examining this chain of action and reaction, Economy and Levi reveal China's acquisition of resources to be a less straightforward and coherent process than generally painted in the media. For instance, while Chinese companies enjoy the benefits of commercial diplomacy and low-cost financing, they do not entirely follow directions from Beijing, and are as much driven by profitability, and pressure from foreign governments, the mass media and public.

The authors have also found little indication that there is a dominant strategy of resource acquisition from Beijing, not least because global trade and investments, particularly in commodities, have anchored practices that are not easily swayed by new entrants, even one with formidable purchasing power. China is, in addition, also increasingly benchmarking itself to global standards and practices, and placing more trust in global markets.

The book dispels other myths, including the fact that China is not the largest investor in the resource world by far, ranking third in southeast Asia, fourth in Africa, and third in Latin America. Some arguments, however, are less convincing. Attempting to place China's appetite for resources in context, the book suggests that it should not be alarming that China, which accounts for 20% of the world population is consuming, 10% of the global oil supply. But this low per capita consumption can only be set to grow as the country's drive towards urbanization is likely to lead to even higher consumption of resources in the near future that can only be partially offset by improved efficiency and resource diversification.

It is undeniable that the staggering increase in China's demand for resources has had some negative effects, particularly in labor practices, corruption, environmental degradation, and coupled with China's embroilment in several territorial disputes, also raises concerns on continued freedom of navigation in key maritime channels.

But Economy and Levi offer a timely reminder that the Chinese enterprises are not that different from multinational companies from other developing countries (not, as they are quick to emphasize, that this makes some of the less-than-ideal practices more acceptable), and new technology, improved efficiency in energy use, resource diversification, strengthened governance in resource-rich countries and their participation in international accords such as the Extractive Industries Transparency Initiative are likely to set in motion a virtuous circle.

As the authors rationally point out, this is the scenario all parties should strive towards, rather than focus on fears and alarmist rhetoric on China's demand for resources, a state of affairs that is here to stay.

By All Means Necessary: How China's Resource Quest Is Changing the World, Elizabeth Economy, Michael Levi (Oxford University Press, USA, February 2014)

The Opium War: Drugs, Dreams and the Making of China by Julia Lovell

reviewed by Peter Gordon

31 August 2014 — Julia Lovell's "immensely readable" account has (finally) been released in an American edition. Here is our review from October 2011:

* * *

The Opium War never figured very highly in Western historical consciousness, and indeed today is all but forgotten, but it is still very much at the forefront of Chinese national and official self-awareness. Julia Lovell writes in her new history of the Sino-British conflict that

> In China today, the Opium War is the traumatic inauguration of the country's modern history. History books, television documentaries and museums chorus a simple, received wisdom about the conflict ... now one of the founding myths of Chinese nationalism. In the century and a half since it was fought, the Opium War has been transformed from a mere 'border provocation' into the tragic beginning of China's modern history...

China's past isn't dead; to paraphrase Faulkner, it isn't even past. After 170 years, the Opium War, the episode that launched China's modern history, still informs contemporary China policy and bedevils international relations:

> From the age of opium traders to the Internet, China and the West have been infuriating and misunderstanding each other, despite ever-increasing opportunities for contact, study and mutual sympathy. Ten years into the twentieth-century, the nineteenth is still with us.

Anyone who has spent any time in Hong Kong (a place which, after all, owes its very existence to the Opium War) will have heard the story many times over: British merchants, demonstrating a streak of deplorable cynicism (or commercial innovation, depending on one's point of view), hit upon opium as the must-have consumer product that would plug the huge trade deficit with China. By the 1830s, silver—the only mutually acceptable medium of exchange—was flowing out of China at what had become an unacceptable rate. When the Chinese authorities set about destroying stocks of this illegal import which was destabilizing their economy and undermining their society, Britain invaded, guns blazing. It demanded and received compensation and, perhaps worse, extra-territorial concessions.

Lovell takes us through the Opium War blow-by-blow and communiqué-by-communiqué, a thorough account that benefits from being immensely readable. In addition to her accomplishments as a historian, Lovell was first recognized as one of the leading translators of contemporary Chinese fiction. Her ear for dialogue and character is well in evidence here. She quotes extensively from contemporary materials and sources. As she tells the story, the protagonists speak in their own voices, from the unfortunate Charles Elliot and the ineffectual Qing Emperor Daoguang to the German missionary turned spymaster and magistrate, Karl Gützlaff. In one extraordinary and almost touching passage, Lovell refers to a letter from Daoguang:

> Two and a half years after the war was supposed to have started, Donguang found himself still lacking the most information about his antagonists: where, in fact, he wondered in a communication of May 1842, is England? Why are the English selling us opium? What are Indians doing in their army? How is it they have a twenty-two-year-old woman for a queen? Is she married?

It may be that the tides of history, throwing the irresistible force of British-led economic globalization against the immovable object of the Qing dynasty's worldview, made conflict inevitable. Lovell's book is a welcome and vivid reminder that history is ultimately made by people.

One might question today whether the Opium War needs additional explanation: even the staunchest apologists for the Empire find it impossible to justify armed intervention to support the drug trade. The establishment of Hong Kong, and its on-the-whole benign existence since its foundation, is perhaps the only silver lining to this account. The higher principle on which the British sent in their warships was not the defense of free-trade so much as the freedom to deal in narcotics. A large segment of the British public has always been suitably embarrassed, albeit not embarrassed enough to have relinquished Hong Kong until the last possible moment.

Lovell is at pains to point out that the narrative is more nuanced than that. While providing no excuse for the aggression, opium wasn't exactly forced upon the Chinese users, and was imported with the cooperation of Chinese merchants and officials. China produced large amounts of the drug itself. Neither nation was in full control, or in much control at all, or often even aware, of what was happening commercially in Canton. The Emperor's officials lied to him and communications were so slow in those pre-telegraph days that events quickly outran decisions. Lovell notes

> how much of the venom in the Chinese version of these events is reserved for characters on their own side: and in particular, for the perceived corruption, indecision and incompetence of the Qing court.

* * *

The final third of *The Opium War* deals with the aftermath, a period which extends to the present. The Second Opium War, a reprise of the first a decade and a half later, is dealt with briskly. Lovell then argues that the Opium War, or rather the passions it stirred up, mutated into deep-set prejudices and attitudes. Lovell draws a line from these events to the "Yellow Peril" and Sax Rohmer's Mystery of Dr Fu Manchu. She dates the current Chinese view of the Opium War to the 1920s:

> The aim was to persuade the populace to blame all China's problems on a single foreign enemy: to transform the Opium War and its Unequal Treaty into a long-term imperialist scheme from which only the Nationalists could preserve the country, thereby justifying any sacrifice that the party required of the Chinese.

* * *

The thoroughness of Lovell's *The Opium War* renders it more thought-provoking than one might at first suppose. This was not, for example, the first "almost accidental" military action by the British to become part of another nation's national mythology. Americans grow up, as I did, with stories of the Boston Massacre, a relatively minor event thoroughly propagandized by the revolutionaries. America now seems, on the whole, to be able to separate the actions of the historically perfidious Albion from the modern nation and its people. China apparently hasn't, or won't; at least not yet.

A related realization is that one country's defining event is another's sidebar. (I recall being astounded, during my year at a London grammar school, that what I knew as the "War of 1812" was considered little more than a minor police action related to the Napoleonic Wars.) The Opium War hardly figures in British historical consciousness. Americans and other Western nations forget that they ever had a role in the opium trade at all. This asymmetry in national memory surely accounts for much of the recurring miscomprehension.

Also thrown into relief are the parallels between the mid-19th century and today. China is once again running a huge trade surplus; the West hasn't yet found its 21st-century equivalent of opium. After a period of ideological conflict, the West's problems with China are, once again, related to trade and deficits. And once again, a potentially mutually-beneficial relationship based on trade and investment, rather than the deep antagonism of earlier decades, is bedeviled by misunderstanding.

Lovell believes that the similarities are more than coincidental:

> In 1839 the Qing court was too distracted by fears of social unrest to come up voluntarily with a pragmatic response to Western trade demands; Britain interpreted this political paralysis as inveterate xenophobia. In 2010, the situation did not look so very different, with the government infuriating Western states over its rejection of climate-change legislation that might slow growth, its harsh stance on social control and its aversion to compromise on international-trade issues, such as strengthening the yuan relative to the dollar...

The differences, of course, are just as stark: China, this time, is in the ascendant, and Western nations are no longer in a position to impose their views on international trade by force, military or economic.

China's views on a number of subjects, including its suspicion of contemporary Western motives, become easier to understand, or at least more nuanced, when seen through the prism of the Opium War. Western protestations on everything from human rights to trade policy acquire a sheen of disingenuousness when compared with their statements of a century and a half ago justifying military and economic aggression. Lovell writes:

> Influential nineteenth-century Britons worked hard to fabricate a virtuous casus belli out of an elementary problem of a trade deficit: to reinvent the war as a clash of civilizations triggered by the 'unnaturally' isolationist Chinese.

China has not forgotten. This is not to excuse disingenuousness on the part of China, nor is it to argue that China is necessarily well-served by its insistence on allowing this monochromatic view of the past to color its present relations. However, Western policy-makers and commentators would do well to make an effort to remember whence China's views on international relations arise.

The Opium War: Drugs, Dreams and the Making of Modern China, Julia Lovell (Overlook Press, August 2014; Pan MacMillan, September 2011)

The Emperor Far Away: Travels at the Edge of China by David Eimer

reviewed by Tim Hannigan

25 August 2014 — According to a Chinese proverb "the mountains are high and the Emperor far away." Thought to date from the time of the Yuan Dynasty, the proverb conveys a sense of distant borderlands, operating on their own terms and untroubled by imperial decrees. Given this original implication, it is a strangely inappropriate source for the title of David Eimer's new book. During Eimer's travels in China's remote borderlands in *The Emperor Far Away* there is often a sense that the Chinese authorities—Republican replacement for the Emperor of old—are if anything too close for comfort.

* * *

China can appear monolithic and mono-ethnic to outsiders. But in fact there are an estimated 100 million non-Han Chinese citizens, members of no fewer than 55 officially recognized ethnic minorities (and countless smaller groups lacking the minimum 5,000 members, writes Eimer, required for official recognition). In this book, Eimer—a British journalist based in Beijing from 2005 to 2012—sets out to explore the peripheral regions where many of these minorities live: Xinjiang and Tibet in the west; Yunnan in the south; and Dongbei in the far northeast:

> places where nationality is a nebulous concept, where the passport a person possesses is less important than their ethnicity.

In his introduction Eimer declares that

> Giving the different ethnic groups a voice—something mostly denied them

> in China itself—while journeying to some of the least-known corners of the world to do so is the principal motivation for this book.

It's a lofty goal, and though he isn't always successful in achieving it, he certainly takes his readers on a thoroughly enjoyable journey in the process.

The first half of the book takes in Xinjiang and Tibet, the minority regions which receive most attention from foreigners, and the places where the discontent of some indigenous people with Chinese rule is most visible to outsiders. These are the places where China looks most like a colonial power, with the local Uighurs and Tibetans clearly distinct from the Han Chinese in culture, lifestyle and language.

Xinjiang and Tibet are also places where indiscreet conversations with inquisitive foreigners are not taken lightly, given the strong presence of the Chinese security forces. It's little surprise, then, that Eimer—making fairly brief visits and speaking, by his own admission, only English and "bad Mandarin"—doesn't manage to delve particularly deep beneath the surface. Instead, he mostly falls back on the role of a traditional travel writer. He takes road trips and writes compellingly about the harsh landscapes; he hangs around in bars and smokes cannabis with foreign backpackers; he enjoys a romantic dalliance with a TV producer from Beijing; and he tells tales of the European explorers who traversed these regions in the 19th century.

This is all great fun, but it's not entirely original. The desert road that Eimer travels from Xinjiang to Qinghai might be far from most tourist itineraries, but it's a well-beaten track for travel writers, and everyone from Peter Fleming and Ella Maillart in the 1930s to Nick Danziger and William Dalrymple in the 1980s and Colin Thubron more recently has passed this way. The pilgrimage route around Mount Kailash in Tibet, meanwhile, is standard adventure travel magazine fodder.

Eimer has clearly done prior research, and he serves up lots of pithy historical nuggets along the way. And he has an impressive knack for the telling analogy: the scale of Han migration to Xinjiang in the last half-century, he writes, is for Uighurs

> the equivalent of 25 million Poles arriving in the UK, or 120 million Mexicans migrating to the USA, and taking charge of the economy, while refusing to employ the natives and demanding they learn to speak Polish or Spanish.

He is also refreshingly frank in describing his own negative reactions to Tibet and Tibetans in a manner that echoes the searing honesty of Peter Hessler's *River Town*. But ultimately you'll find more meaningful insight on Xinjiang and Tibet elsewhere.

* * *

It is in the second half of *The Emperor Far Away* that Eimer is much more original and impressive. Readers who have been enjoying the travelogue ride in Xinjiang and Tibet may be disappointed by the change of pace as Eimer descends first on Yunnan, home to half of China's officially recognized minorities, and then on the chilly reaches of Dongbei, where China borders Russia and North Korea, for he slows the pace and focuses much less on his own journey in these places. But in doing so he comes up with plenty of fresh insight, and does indeed succeed in giving a voice to some of the people he meets.

Some of the chapters here have the feel of recycled journalism—an investigation of the Burmese women trafficked across the Yunnan border into China or meetings with evangelical Christians and North Korean immigrants in the northeast. But they are among the strongest parts of *The Emperor Far Away*, with Eimer's skill as a journalist on full display. A surreptitious trip from Yunnan into Myanmar's Wa State, meanwhile—culminating in a gonzo-style account of a heroin- and methamphetamine-fueled night on the tiles with a rebel general's son—is one of the most memorable sections in the whole book.

The subtle ethnic situation in Yunnan and Dongbei is markedly less suited to black-and-white portrayals than Xinjiang and Tibet, and Eimer identifies plenty of nuances. In these places, various groups live together alongside members of the Han majority in a complex ethnic mosaic, with tensions and between minorities as likely to feature as resentment of the

Han. In the tropical Xishuangbanna region of southern Yunnan, Eimer describes the animosity that smaller tribal minorities often feel for the Dai, the largest minority in the region, because of their apparent wealth.

The Dai, Eimer feels, are a minority that has successfully negotiated a role in a powerful, Han-dominated Chinese state, providing Han Chinese tourists with "a diluted, utterly unthreatening glimpse of their traditional lifestyle" and offering the authorities "a dream of how a subservient ethnic group should act." This makes for a striking contrast with the unhappy lot of Uighurs and Tibetans:

> By acquiescing in the Chinese appropriation of the most superficial aspects of their culture for the tourist trade, they have created some room in which to preserve their fundamental uniqueness in the face of the increasing Han presence...

* * *

In the final part of the book, Eimer travels to the chilly northern reaches of Dongbei, the northeastern region made up of Heilongjiang, Liaoning, and Jilin provinces, a region where the Manchu and other minorities have largely assimilated with the Han, and where there are few of the tensions of the Tibet or Xinjiang on display.

This is also, Eimer suggests, a region where China's reach is extending beyond its current boundaries.

The book ends with refreshing understatement: there is no portentously reflective epilogue; instead Eimer simply crosses the Amur River into the bleak and impoverished Russian Far East, looks back to the south, and feels "the neon lights of Heihe calling me towards China."

In the earlier sections of the book Eimer has crossed other borders, into Kazakhstan and Kyrgyzstan from Xinjiang, and into Laos and Myanmar from Yunnan, apparently to highlight how the minorities of the Chinese peripheries have more in common with their ethnic cousins in neighboring countries than with the Han majority.

But something else is implied in this final crossing to a region where the economic influence of China is increasingly felt. The "Emperor" is no longer far away in the Chinese outlands, and for the local minorities the assimilation of the Manchu or the negotiation of the Dai offer better prospects than the resistance of Uighurs and Tibetans. What's more, no matter how high the mountains or great the distance from Beijing, Chinese power and influence is reaching beyond boundaries to make its presence felt amongst other minorities in the borderlands of other nations.

Emperor Far Away; Travels at the Edge of China, David Eimer (Bloomsbury Publishing, August 2014)

Eastern Fortress: A Military History of Hong Kong, 1840-1970 by Kwong Chi Man and Tsoi Yiu Lun

reviewed by Bill Purves

24 August 2014 — Hong Kong's history as a fortress can be briefly summarized as a century and a half of mercifully somnolent garrison duty interrupted in 1941 by two weeks of furious combat. The co-authors of *Eastern Fortress* divide their work accordingly, with both contributing to the long, long chapter on the invasion (about a quarter of the text), and Kwong Chi Man covering the rest.

Many authors have recounted the story of the invasion, but Tsoi and Kwong seem to have made some new contributions by spending much more time working with Japanese sources. They present a reasonably balanced account of the preparations and the fighting, analyzing developments from both the invaders' and the defenders' points of view. Even those who feel themselves pretty familiar with the story will probably learn something new from his treatment.

The longer section by Kwong reads like another book entirely. His treatment of the early decades from 1840 to 1915 describes a long series of tactical and strategic plans, most of which were never adopted, supplemented by endless detail about the deployment, upgrading and redeployment of artillery, none of which was ever fired in anger. His approach is strictly chronological, which makes important themes almost impossible to follow. Even changes in the size of the garrison, rather fundamental data, are almost impossible to follow when the figures are referred to only sporadically in the course of the chronology. Kwong is clear that malaria and venereal disease made Hong Kong a highly dangerous posting in the early decades, but again the data supporting him are scattered through the story, making them difficult to understand.

Kwong does, however, explain very clearly the irony of the book's title. Until 1914, Hong Kong was indeed the eastern fortress of the British Empire. It was the Royal Navy's principal base and depot, and it remained impregnable as long as Britannia ruled the waves in the Far East. The navy's offense was the colony's defense. With the First World War the fleet was withdrawn to Europe, and in the war's aftermath, with the Great Depression, it was never able to return. Britain simply couldn't afford it.

Kwong then explains that when the treaty of alliance between Britain and Japan expired in 1922, Hong Kong immediately morphed from a fortress into an "exposed outpost". Britain's military planners acknowledged that,

> Militarily our position in the Far East would be stronger without this unsatisfactory commitment.

It was maintained primarily as a matter of imperial prestige. The army's main role

> … was to project an image of strength through parades and other imperial ceremonies, such as the arrival and departure of governors.

> Maintaining face by holding Hong Kong [was] an important rationale for generations of policymakers.

But everyone realized it was indefensible.

Fortress status was reprised from 1942 to 1945 as long as the Japanese navy and air force controlled the South China Sea. But the authors seem not to have delved into the Japanese sources on that period. Kwong describes Hong Kong's role as a major supply depot and naval base in general terms, but provides no details about what actually went on.

After the war, Hong Kong became a fortress in another sense. Modern longer-range weapons and the Cold War created for everyone an era of instant, push-button apocalypse. Technically, Hong Kong was even less defensible than ever; but as things worked out it prospered throughout the

Cold War as a relatively safe haven. Britain could go to war in Egypt and Argentina, the People's Republic of China could go to war with India and Vietnam, but through it all it was difficult to imagine an enemy wanting to antagonize both Britain and China simultaneously by attacking Hong Kong.

Kwong either fails to understand that, or he has willfully ignored it despite the fact that it fits his fortress theme well.

Along with Berlin and Vienna, fortress Hong Kong delivered great value to all sides as a cockpit of international espionage. Kwong mentions that, and he provides a few very sketchy examples, but little solid history. Most of the records of that activity probably remain secret today, but rather than acknowledge that difficulty, Kwong skates around the entire issue.

So *Eastern Fortress* comprises several very contrasting parts. Its strength is its clear account of the development of Hong Kong's strategic role over the decades. Many will also consider valuable its treatment of the invasion from a Japanese perspective. The four chapters of artillery redeployments are likely to seem long to most readers. The treatment of Hong Kong's Cold War role, like that early artillery, is mostly well wide of the mark.

Eastern Fortress: A Military History of Hong Kong, 1840-1970, Kwong Chi Man, Tsoi Yiu Lun (Hong Kong University Press, November 2014)

Betrayal in Paris: How the Treaty of Versailles Led to China's Long Revolution by Paul French

reviewed by Peter Gordon

18 August 2014 — Penguin China's series of brief 100-page "Specials" covering China and World War One is a marvelous initiative; of a strong collection, Paul French's *Betrayal in Paris* may be the most thought-provoking to date.

The story is relatively simple: China believed, due to promises it felt it had been made as well as common sense, that the pre-War German concessions would be returned to China following Germany's defeat. Japan had however seized them and was determined to keep them which, after some sharp-elbowed diplomacy at the Paris Peace Conference about the so-called "Shantung question", it managed to do.

French has considerable facility with narrative description and brings the Chinese delegation to Paris vividly to life. The relatively young and dapper Wellington Koo unofficially led the delegation which bunked down at the Hôtel Lutetia, where they "entertained lavishly, and nightly." Koo, it was generally reckoned, soundly defeated his Japanese counterparts in the debate over the Shantung question—his days on the Columbia debate team paying off—and won the battle for public opinion. He memorably argued that

> leaving Japan in control of Shantung would be like leaving 'a dagger pointed at the heart of China'.

None of it mattered, though. The Japanese took the discussion behind the scenes and made deals. Even at the time, this was considered a betrayal by many in the West as well as, of course, by the Chinese. The fact that American President Woodrow Wilson had let them down—he had told them "You can count on me"—affected the Chinese deeply. China refused to sign the treaty.

The consequences in China notably included the May 4th Movement and all that followed. "The Treaty of Versailles" says the book's subtitle, "Led to China's Long Revolution". French does not quite argue that this alone gave rise to an anti-Western Communist China; it might have happened anyway. Nor were the Chinese singled out for ill treatment—the Arabs, if anything, came off worse, the consequences of which still roil the region a century later.

There are several take-aways from this account. One is how relatively cosmopolitan the Chinese diplomats were. Koo had attended Columbia; he received a PhD in international law and diplomacy. Lou Tseng-tsiang, the nominal head of the delegation, was fluent in English, Russian and French, married to a Belgian and was a Christian (and later became Dom Pierre Célestin in a Bruges Monastery after the War). CT Wang was a graduate of the University of Michigan and Yale Law; he was also Phi Beta Kappa. Alfred Tse was a Cornell grad, in fact the first Chinese Cornell grad. This level of international educational exposure and Western cultural savoir-faire is in considerable contrast to the modern Chinese Foreign Ministry (although with the numbers of Chinese now studying abroad, it may return).

The perhaps less obvious take-away is the parallel to the Diaoyu/Senkaku issue bedevilling intra-Asian relations today. Books only rarely move the needle for me on current affairs, but *Betrayal in Paris* did. Shantung was left in Japanese hands due to the legacy of world conflict, some secret treaties and other agreements which the Chinese were not party to. The Diaoyus/Senkakus are also arguably in Japanese hands due to the legacy of world war and some treaties and agreements from which the Chinese feel excluded. This does not change my position on the issue (which is that history is not very helpful in determining a resolution) and the analogy isn't perfect, but I could now at least understand if the Chinese position was in some way informed by a sense of déjà vu.

The combination of *Betrayal in Paris*'s brevity, French's smooth, easy-to-read prose and the thought-provoking implications would make it an excellent text for stimulating debate in regional history and politics classes. The debate won't always be comfortable, but good debates rarely are.

Betrayal in Paris: How the Treaty of Versailles Led to China's Long Revolution, Paul French (Penguin China, July 2014)

The Mongol Empire: Genghis Khan, His Heirs and the Founding of Modern China by John Man

reviewed by Peter Gordon

13 August 2014 — Those who have already read John Man's *Genghis Khan*, *Xanadu*, *Kublai Khan* and even *The Leadership Secrets of Genghis Khan* might be able to skip his latest offering *The Mongol Empire*, for it covers much the same ground. It does however cover it in fewer pages and provides the entire history in a single, coherent narrative.

The story of the Mongols is endlessly fascinating. Genghis alone, to say of nothing of his heirs, conquered an empire the scope of which the world had never seen before—"four times the size of Alexander's, and twice the size of Rome's"—and he did so, unlike Alexander or the Caesars, from less than even a standing start: he even had a period where his mother, and hence Genghis too, were forced to grub for roots and berries.

Scrape this story—not unlike, in its way, the story of England's King Alfred and the cakes—and one realizes that Genghis's noble blood, for such he had, was that of a tribal chieftain, in effect a herder among herders—a world away from the castles and estates normally associated with kingship and a universe away from what he became. Where, one wonders, did these hordes (itself derived from a Mongol word) of warriors come from?

And, unlike almost all other stories of its kind—from Alexander and Attila to Napoleon and Hitler—the empire not only outlasted the death of the original conqueror but continued to grow: the conquest of China, Tibet, Russia, the Caucasus, and the Levant were still to come. By the standards of Rome, China, and even the Ottomans, the Mongol Empire was short-lived, but it was no mere flash in the night.

The Mongols were religiously tolerant: animists, Buddhists, Muslims,

Daoists and Christians—Kublai's mother was Christian—all rubbed shoulders, relatively conflict-free, in Mongol domains. The Mongols were innovative administrators and absorbed talent from the entire continent: Nepalese architects, Persian engineers and European metalsmiths all found gainful and indeed enthusiastic employment.

Yet the Mongols also slaughtered entire cities—*pour encourager les autres*—and engaged in what today would be called genocide.

John Man, as always, tells the story very well: the 350 pages zip along. He manages to be accurate—paying attention to sources, acknowledging when the information is less than perfect—without ever being dry. He has a way with imagery:

> In fast-forward, the map of Chinese history looks a cell-culture dividing, growing, dying back, but always a plurality...

and with words: as the Mongols seized the walls of Baghdad, Man writes, using less-than-technical but oh-so-evocative language, that

> Panic reduced the caliph to mush.

Man is as much a travel writer as a historian—his interest in Mongolia and its people is clearly very personal. In this book, he keeps his natural predilection for personal anecdote largely in check—with some difficulty, one senses—until the few pages where he gives in and relates stories of some journeys to Mongolia and people he met there. These include investigations into Genghis Khan's final resting place, a mystery which still animates entire populations.

The latter part of the book also includes a fascinating discussion that Man starts by asking

> Given that empires change civilizations, what other effects of Genghis's empire remain today?

Not much, he concludes:

> In Europe, the Romans left vast amounts of hardware — roads, building, aqueducts, stadia — but they also rewrote Europe's software: language, art, literature, law ...

It is not, he writes, just that the Mongols' reign was relatively brief at 150 years.

> Alexander flashed across the skies of history like a comet, yet he left a lasting light. The British were in India for 200 years and the cultures are still interfused.

"Why?" Man writes that

> the Romans, the Greeks and the British had something to say... The Mongols didn't.

Man plays the discussion out over the next dozen pages, comparing the Mongols with the Arabs, bringing in everything from multi-culturalism to movable type, and asking what might have been.

Where the book is a slight disappointment is that it doesn't really achieve the promise of its subtitle: "the founding of modern China". Man points out the more or less straightforward, albeit always surprising, fact that the boundaries of modern China, including Yunnan, Tibet and parts of what is Central Asia, owe almost everything to the Mongol Empire. Kublai moved his capital to Beijing; he established the Chinese Yuan Dynasty of which his grandfather Genghis was posthumously made founder. Man relates the incongruity of it all—including using history to assert, as sometimes happens, Chinese sovereignty over modern Mongolia:

> Officially, no one talks of repudiating the status quo. Unofficially, there is a wrong to be righted. If this ever comes to pass, it will be done in the name, naturally, of Genghis Khan, because it was his heirs who gave China

its present borders (minus Mongolia itself, and a bit of Manchuria, now Russian).

But Man doesn't engage in much analysis. Perhaps there isn't much to be said. Logic, historical or otherwise, rarely rules sovereignty discussions.

And before Westerners express too much superiority over the twisted thought-processes that make Genghis and Kublai into Chinese emperors so as to justify the absorption of their Mongolian conquests into historical and hence modern China, it's worth casting an eye to the current debate over Scottish independence and the upcoming referendum. Britain owes its borders to James VI, King of Scotland, who became England's James I. In earlier centuries, England's claims to large bits and on occasion the entirety of France—the basis for centuries of conflict—also arose from the former's conquest by the Normans.

* * *

The Mongol Empire is a fine book and an enjoyable read. Although Man has covered much of the same material before, here he does so here in one integrated volume.

The Mongol Empire: Genghis Khan, His Heirs and the Founding of Modern China, John Man (Transworld Publishers Ltd, June 2014)

Tibet: An Unfinished Story by Lezlee Brown Halper and Stefan Halper

reviewed by Sinead Ferris

11 August 2014 — *Tibet: An Unfinished Story* opens with a puzzlingly detailed description of American President Franklin D Roosevelt's wartime retreat in the Catoctin Mountains of Maryland. He named it Shangri-La, after the peaceful mountain kingdom in James Hilton's 1933 novel Lost Horizon, said to be inspired by Tibet. This seemingly incongruous passage telegraphs the book's contents better than the title.

Tibet's status is a complex and globally divisive issue that has been approached from many different angles, with widely varying results. Authors Lezlee Brown Halper and Stefan Halper write not so much about Tibet, but about American foreign policy towards Tibet: its motivations, determinants, and limitations.

The FDR anecdote is indicative of the focus in the first half of the book on Tibet's public relations position in the United States, a uniquely positive one among peoples fighting for self-determination. The West's fascination with Tibet is traced by the authors as far back as 500 BC, highlighting ideas of Tibet's isolation and mysticism that frame America's Tibet policy even today.

The authors' in-depth explanation of the inner workings of the American security establishment and administration is fascinating for anyone interested in the twists and turns of diplomatic decision-making. Viewing Tibet from an American perspective allows the authors to situate Tibet's struggle for independence among the big themes of modern history. India-Pakistan relations, the Communist-Nationalist conflict in China, the Cold War, the Korean War, McCarthyism, post-colonial Commonwealth politics, all influenced US policy towards Tibet. One of the book's strengths is this linking of America's broader global struggles to their indirect effects on Tibetan autonomy.

Together with government and historical material, the authors make use of letters and interviews of key participants from the time, resulting in a history that is about personalities as well as politics. The authors' meticulous research is evident and the wealth of anecdotes and asides make for an account as lively as it is thorough.

While there is no denying the important role of the United States vis à vis Tibet, the almost exclusive focus on this angle risks oversimplifying Tibetan history and in particular underplays the roles played by the other principal actors: China, India and Tibet itself.

The authors' portrayals of non-American actors are largely one-dimensional. India is portrayed as obstructionist and naive, Tibet is weak and confused, China is duplicitous. The detail that is so abundant on everything from American government policies, opinions and relationships to preferences, personalities and delegations only highlights the limited coverage of the other participants. Such complex and important issues as the India's complicated relationship with the Tibetan "government-in-exile" and the Chinese perspective—essential in a tale of "competing narratives" about Tibet—are covered only briefly.

More problematically, the choices made by Tibetans are notably absent from a book that aims to tell Tibet's (unfinished) story. Indeed, Tibet comes across as but a peripheral player in its own history. Divisions within the Tibetan government are mentioned as one impediment to Tibetan independence, but neither this concept nor the steps Tibetans have taken to seek independence are explored in detail. Very few of Tibet's key actors, groups, personalities—even the Panchen Lama, the highest figure of Tibetan authority after the Dalai Lama—are covered in much depth.

As a result, *Tibet: An Unfinished Story* paints the US-Tibet relationship as the defining one in Tibetan history, the subtext being that—had the United States been more proactive or less constrained by circumstance—Tibet would be independent today. This conclusion, along with the authors' "hope that Washington would fully commit to Tibetan independence" is a natural one to draw from the narrative presented.

However, wider perspectives show historical and contemporary impediments to independence that do not involve America. This book is an engaging and useful account of American foreign policy towards Tibet and India throughout the twentieth century, but it is worth remembering that there is more to Tibet's story.

Tibet; An Unfinished Story, Lezlee Brown Halper, Stefan Halper (C Hurst & Co Publishers Ltd, November 2013; Oxford University Press, April 2014)

GETTING STUCK IN FOR SHANGHAI

ROBERT BICKERS

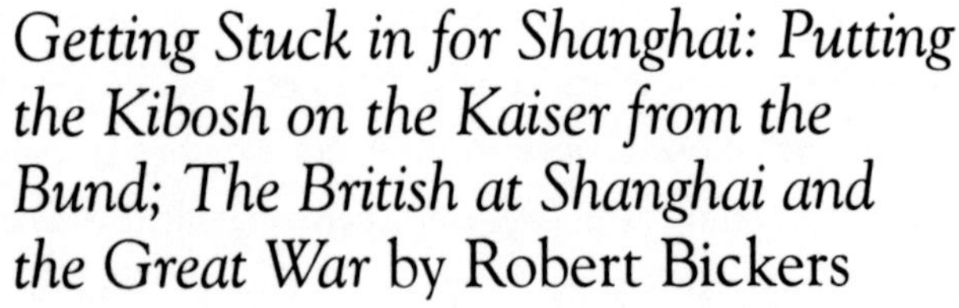

Getting Stuck in for Shanghai: Putting the Kibosh on the Kaiser from the Bund; The British at Shanghai and the Great War by Robert Bickers

reviewed by Peter Gordon

2 August 2014 — *Getting Stuck in for Shanghai* by Robert Bickers is another in the appealing Penguin China series of 100-odd page "Specials" on China and World War One. This particular volume covers the British "Shanghai-landers" that went back to Europe to fight.

Bickers, as those who have read *Empire Made Me*—his full-length biography of Shanghai policeman Maurice Tinkler—may already know, is able to master both primary sources such as personal letters and contemporary newspaper accounts as well as the contemporary zeitgeist—a term I am using without irony in spite of the subject matter. The tone of this book is telegraphed by its subtitle: "Putting the Kibosh on the Kaiser from the Bund".

This was not a terribly significant factor in the First World War. The soldiers numbered in the hundreds, fewer—one imagines—than from a moderately-sized town in Britain. Their stories from the front, captured in letters, are as stiff-upper-lip and horrific as any, but not hugely different from others' one reads elsewhere. The interest in the book, beside Bickers's skill at portraiture and finding the telling anecdote, lies in the tussle he depicts between patriotism and Shanghai's "cosmopolitanism":

> Shanghai also stood out, the foreigners felt, as a paragon of modern cosmopolitanism. A memorial to the shipwrecked crew of the German gunboat the Iltis stood on Jardine-Matheson-owned land at the entrance the Public Gardens, permission for which was granted 'with much pleasure' by the company... The Germans of the Club Concordia returned such favours. They hosted the British members of the Shanghai Club during the years

when the Shanghai Club was being rebuilt...

The British had always gotten along pretty well the Germans in Shanghai:

> they played, marched, raced, rowed, sang and celebrated together... They founded companies together and sat side by side on boards of directors and sports clubs committees.

The people most British really worried about, when they weren't worrying about the Chinese, were the Japanese.

This convivial fabric started to fray when War broke out:

> American journalist John Powell later recalled how Britons and Germans would cut each other as they strolled to their respective clubs.

Men shipped off to war, women patriotically knitted socks, the Germans sank the Lusitania, and Germans, at least in the view of those on the front, became the Bosches.

One might today smirk at a life centered on Clubs—the Germans were ultimately allowed back in; "they were gentlemen after all"—but the Shanghai of the foreign concessions, for all its imperialism and colonialism, seemed to manage its disputes, at least among its constituent communities, better than did the nations whence they hailed.

Getting Stuck in for Shanghai: Putting the Kibosh on the Kaiser from the Bund; The British at Shanghai and the Great War, Robert Bickers (Penguin China, May 2014)

Age of Ambition: Chasing Fortune, Truth and Faith in the New China by Evan Osnos

reviewed by
Jonathan Chatwin

17 July 2014 — It has become commonplace in commentary on China to qualify one's observations with an acknowledgement that the country's scale and pace of change precludes the articulation of any coherent, overarching narrative. Accounts of the country tend now—and not without good reason—to focus on evaluating specific aspects of the culture, society, economy or political system, or to tease out anecdotal insight through individual portraits.

Given its epochal title and physical heft, Evan Osnos's *Age of Ambition* suggests at first glance that it may buck this trend, and advance a "Key to All Mythologies" for 21st century China. To some extent, this expectation is rewarded; this is certainly a book which deals with big ideas, most fundamentally the tension that exists between the increasing specific freedoms—social, artistic, economic, romantic—now available to the Chinese citizen, and the authoritarianism that continues to define the overall parameters of their lives.

Osnos sees this tension as the possible source, eventually, of the ruling party's demise, observing, by the book's end, a feeling of fragility that has taken hold in China. In the prologue and epilogue to *Age of Ambition*, Osnos teases out parallels between the China of this new millennium and the America of the late nineteenth century, in which brash confidence masked a nation's institutional and social immaturity. Osnos quotes Fitzgerald's observation of the misguided faith held by that archetypal American dreamer, Jay Gatsby, in the "promise that the rock of the world was founded securely on a fairy's wing." America and Gatsby came to realize the insecurity of those foundations; will China be forced to a similar understanding in the decade to come?

However, the questions posed by *Age of Ambition* find a response not in any grand, overarching thesis, but rather in individual stories of Chinese life. The national narrative, Osnos observes in the work's prologue, is "splintering into a billion stories—stories of flesh and blood, of idiosyncracies and solitary struggles."

Osnos is a journalist by trade, and spent eight years (from 2005 to 2013) in China as a reporter for both the *Chicago Tribune* and the *New Yorker.* He is a skilled cataloguer of the personal, able to get beyond the superficial layers of formality which are inherent in Chinese discourse, and which often prove challenging for outsiders to penetrate.

The book interweaves these stories through three thematic sections looking, respectively, at the role of money ("Fortune"), information ("Truth") and political and social structures ("Faith") in modern China. *Age of Ambition* is certainly a remarkable work of synthesis, deftly switching between the macro and micro, the national and the personal, as it moves through these sections, layering and filling a vivid portrait of a country in an astonishing state of flux.

Yet, as with all portraits, perspective is limited. To an extent such limitations are an inherent and accepted element of a work such as *Age of Ambition* given both its subject which, as has been noted, tends to resist holistic treatment, and its reliance on partial accounts of the individual. However, there is an artificial limitation evident here, too, a concentration (not total, but significant) on the urban, educated and moneyed: on the exceptions in Chinese society. Osnos sees the narratives of those such as Lin Yifu (former Chief Economist of the World Bank) and Gong Haiyan (founder of online Chinese dating site Jiayuan) as metaphoric of aspects of the new Gilded Age; the question must be asked, however, as to whether stories of such individuals tell us a great deal about the majority experience of living through the "Age of Ambition". The later focus in the work on the political activism of Ai Weiwei, Chen Guangcheng and Liu Xiaobo raises similar questions and, whilst Osnos asserts that understanding the treatment of such dissidents is "vital to understanding China", he is conscious that such individuals are, fundamentally, outliers.

Yet, perhaps the story of a remarkable age requires remarkable protagonists. In telling the story of the American boom, Fitzgerald focused on the rich and the luminous; the great unwashed are hardly glimpsed in *The Great Gatsby*. It took the Wall Street Crash for the true impact of the new American age on its less romantic subjects to come clearly into focus. Whether a similarly revealing moment occurs over the coming years in China, one hopes that Osnos, now returned to America as an east coast correspondent for the *New Yorker*, will continue to focus his gaze on this new Age of Ambition, and will return to tell some more of the billion stories—prosaic and grandiose—that emerge from it.

Age of Ambition; Chasing Fortune, Truth and Faith in the New China, Evan Osnos (Vintage, June 2014; Farrar Straus Giroux, May 2014)

The New Emperors: Power and the Princelings in China by Kerry Brown

reviewed by Peter Gordon

7 July 2014 — Kerry Brown's latest book, *The New Emperors: Power and Princelings in China*, is not quite the broad-brush exposé implied by the title and, especially, subtitle "What Does it Take to Becomes China's Leader"; rather, it is a clear and straightforward introduction to China's current political lineup headed by Xi Jinping—who they are and how they got there.

There are people who find the ins-and-out of politics inherently fascinating; I am not one of them. Other than the top two or three leaders in a country, I can find it hard to keep the people straight. Chinese politics is particularly obscure, which probably increases the appeal for those with a predilection for what used to be known as kremlinology, but that just makes it even harder to follow for the rest of us.

But clear and important don't always correlate; perhaps they rarely do. Those of us who don't understand what is going on in China should take heart, however: it seems we are not alone. Brown writes in relation to Bo Xilai's fall from grace that

> One of the most striking aspects of the Bo case ... was the way it showed how we, observers, analysts, and those generally interested in politics in the world's second largest economy and most populous nation, really don't know or understand power in China now.

But Brown is as good a pilot through these cloudy waters as one could wish to have. He steers a careful line between defining the protagonists as personalities—no easy task, given how private these leaders almost invariably are and the levels of secrecy built up around them—and describing the systems and procedures through which they passed. He demonstrates that the resulting leadership is a combination, one that seems uniquely Chinese, of personality and process.

Brown identifies several common threads, patronage and family relationships, for example, and the shared trauma of the Cultural Revolution, that should come as no surprise. He leads with a concise and riveting recap of Bo Xilai's self-destruction.

But much of the strength of the book lies in the numerous pointed observations, for example:

> One of the key skills that has helped Xi in becoming Party leader, beyond patronage and network building, has been management of his relatives...

from which Brown helps the reader draw insights:

> And in a country where refusing the demands of these members of the closest of close networks is one of the toughest issues, it is here that we can see something of Xi's inner values and world.

But perhaps the most revelatory aspect of the book—something that might be obvious in retrospect, but nevertheless missable in a forest-and-trees way—is how different China is from any other political system that comes to mind.

Although China uses much of the same language and outward form of the old USSR—the Communist Party, Politburo, etc.—it is now so different as to be largely unrecognizable. Chinese leaders now have fixed terms of office and step down when those terms are up.

There is, furthermore, very much a political process: it is not a system (again, any longer) dominated by individual strongmen. Brown describes a leadership based on alliances and relationships built up over decades, horse-trading and if not necessarily compromise, then papered-over differences. It is, he says, a "networked leadership". Perhaps as a result, it does not seem—as authoritarian regimes have often been—to be very brittle.

Furthermore, according to Brown, the explicitly political aspects of the process have been strengthening:

> The Eighteenth Party Congress [the one that brought in the current leadership] was the final outcome of a process in which political, not factional or patronage, issues were decisive... There were family and patron ingredients, and they did factor — but not decisively. We have to view the Eighteenth Party Congress final leadership line-up as a statement of political purpose, and the result of a long and sometimes ferocious argument about where to steer the country in a critical moment of its development.

Projecting analogies from other places on to China may do little to aid understanding and might in fact impede it.

It doesn't hurt that Brown is not just a clear writer but also rather a more literate one than such books typically have. Not only does he reference such contemporary novelists as Chan Koonchung and Yu Hua, but how many China books make reference to Oliver Goldsmith, the eighteenth-century English playwright? The section title "Xi stoops to conquer" is very clever.

Brown takes this vitally important yet inherently obscure subject and makes it about as accessible to the general reader as it could hope to be. His facility with observations in turn perspicacious and piquant, and his ability to turn a felicitous phrase, make *The New Emperors: Power and Princelings in China* an easier read than it might easily have been in less deft hands.

Kerry Brown is a frequent contributor to *The Asian Review of Books*.

The New Emperors; Power and the Party in China, Kerry Brown (I.B.Tauris & Co Ltd, June 2014)

Hard Road Home: Selected Essays by Ye Fu

reviewed by John Butler

5 July 2014 — "Is human cruelty an instinct of our animal nature or a genetic trait?" Ye Fu asks at the beginning of his essay "An Education in Cruelty", and goes on to wonder whether it is "a dysfunction forced on us by a particular kind of society, or does it rise from an individual's education and upbringing?"

China, of course, hasn't got the monopoly on cruelty, but, as Ye Fu shows us, the regimes that followed the fall of the Manchu Empire have been quite creative in their use of it, from Mao's "Great Leap Forward" to the horrors of Tiananmen Square, to cite just two examples, and this collection of essays offers a brilliant exposé of events that led up to the China of 2014. He does not do this by writing a sweeping historical epic, but through essays about ordinary people, some of whom are members of his own family, but all playing their own parts in what Yeats called "the casual comedy".

Ye Fu is the name under which Zheng Shi-ping wrote these essays: it means "the Wild Man", perhaps alluding to the fact that the author cannot be tamed, and that nothing will stop him from exposing the tyranny and cruelty of China's recent past, whilst at the same time holding out a hope that is rooted in Chinese history and the culture of tradition.

Andrew Clark is to be highly commended for translating this book, providing clear and extensive explanatory notes and for making Ragged Banner Press, a small independent company, available as an outlet in the West for authors who face difficulties publishing in their own countries. Clark has enabled Chinese writers to speak out for themselves in their own authentic voices, rather than being interpreted through the prism of the West; here we have a Chinese writer directly addressing Chinese readers (he is currently still in China) and presenting his case according to his own cultural values. Rather than directly or indirectly suggesting that China should be more "westernized", Ye Fu draws on the past as a repository of ideas that might make the present and future in China more humanistic, more thoughtful, less materialistic and less ideologically-driven.

Ye Fu does not look back with simplistic nostalgia for the "good old days" or anything like that, but he sees in the past what the translator Clark calls "his touchstone of goodness", expressed not as "culturally specific traits" but as "human character itself". Ye Fu sees tradition as something which, in spite of all its shortcomings, "breathed decency and integrity", and those qualities are what he still finds even in the holocaust of the terrible events after 1949, qualities symbolized here by members of his own family and by people he encountered on his own "hard road home". This book of essays allows the Wild Man to find out who he and where he might be going, and it is a moving experience indeed to read how he makes his pilgrim's progress. It is also a scathing and depressing picture of China's recent past of war, revolution and repression, serving as a sharp reminder to Western readers that we should not be taken in by the friendly fuzzy face of modern-day China. Western readers need to be informed of what Clark terms the "Machiavellian calculus" which not only brutally disposed of more than a million landowners under Mao Zedong, but which still operates today in many spheres of Chinese life.

A "road home" is actually a "road back", and one aspect of the Chinese experience, as Ye Fu would have us believe, is that there has been a concerted effort by the authorities to make sure that no-one can find that road. Ye Fu, in this book, relates how he looked for his family, and in the first essay, "A Mother to the River Gone", he begins with his mother and her ordeal, which ended ten years previously in "those ice-cold waters" into which she threw herself. She was labelled a "rightist", which, Ye Fu says, means that she had "an uncompromising personality" and could not cut the ties to her own father, who had served the pre-Communist government under Chiang Kai-shek.

Ye Fu presents sketches of others who would not break or bend, such as "Brother Blind Man" and "Su Jiaqiao, a Man Apart" and, in the final poignant essay "Tomb Lantern", Ye Fu's grandmother. The lengthy essay

"Requiem for a Landlord", in which Ye Fu's grandfather figures prominently, chronicles the fall of a family whose sin consisted in owning land, and when Mao unleashed his Cultural Revolution they "were forever pilloried and there was no end to their humiliations."

Even children were enlisted by the Party to inflict humiliations on other children, and spying, betrayal and cruelty abounded in all walks of life. By showing how these various people suffered and endured, Ye Fu erects a monument to the human spirit, which shines out in these essays despite the appalling repression, forced conformity and mindless violence inflicted upon it. The last paragraph of "Tomb Lantern" says it all:

> Each of us has his own story about a loving relative, and buried under every tombstone lies a long tale of cruel suffering. How can the gossamer of the written word bear the weight of that tale, honestly told? Yet if there is no Heaven to receive the souls of the dead, then let the writing of their story be a spiritual settling of accounts, to repay in this life the debts incurred in this life. What else can we do that will have any impact on the world?

China's economic "progress" is lauded in the Western press, and business people, the delights of profit lighting up their faces, are finding endless excuses to cosy up to the gigantic Chinese market that beckons them like a monstrous grinning stuffed panda toy. While China is certainly, at least materially, a "better" place to live for some, much of its material and social progress has been built upon the bodies and blood of its own people. It is sincerely to be hoped that Ye Fu's book will be widely-read and that it will have some impact on the world, which is perhaps too easily blinded by surface appearances and outward posterity.

Hard Road Home: Selected Essays, Ye Fu (Ragged Banner Press, March 2014)

Exploiting Africa: The Influence of Maoist China in Algeria, Ghana, and Tanzania by Donovan C. Chau

reviewed by Kerry Brown

25 June 2014 — Africa and China are becoming hot topics, with a cascade of books in the last couple of years. In the mid-2000s it was hard to find many people who were engaged in this subject. Now the field is becoming crowded.

Donovan C. Chau's contribution, *Exploiting Africa: The Influence of Maoist China*, is different inasmuch as it looks not to the present, but to the past, and in particular to the era 1956-1976 when the People's Republic of China had its first real spate of activity on the continent.

Knowing a bit more about this phase of engagement is a useful antidote to the oft-repeated wisdom of today where many blithely discourse about China's discovery of Africa and its new role there. Some of the things that Chau writes about are eerily similar to today. The use of aid projects to gain political interference, the importation of as many as 70 thousand Chinese to work on Tanzania railway in the late 1960s, the visits by senior Chinese leaders to court African ones and vice versa—all this was occurring from the late 1950s onwards and shadows behavior that China is accused of using in the 21st century.

There were clear differences though, between China's mode of interaction with its numerous countries of interest in west, north and east Africa, and the case studies that Chau uses illustrate this. Much of it was driven by the PRC's desire to get enough votes at the UN to acquire a seat over that of the Republic of China on Taiwan which was occupying it then. This was achieved in 1971.

China was also far more heavily and explicitly engaged with internal politics in some of the countries it was present in, being linked to support for internal revolutions in Algeria where it funded and provided logistics and training the anti-French colonial struggle, and less happily in Ghana and Tanzania, where it got dragged into clashes between post-colonial competitors. Perhaps the unhappy memory of these involvements explains China's wise distancing from most overt contemporary political engagement in Africa. For the 21st century, it is insistent that it is all about material help and commercial partnership rather than supplying ideological support.

As Li Keqiang said during his 2014 tour of several African countries, China is a partner that does not lecture. This prior era of closeness in Africa-Chinese relations with all the headaches it led to must be the basis behind that principle.

This book is clearly a PhD thesis converted to a monograph, and while it has some valuable material from mostly English-languages sources on Maoist China working in Africa, the introduction makes two statements, the first of which is contentious and the second surely wrong, and these inform the rest of the work.

Of the first, Chau claims that China was primarily motivated in these activities in different African states because it was always an aspiring global player. There was certainly an internationalist tone in many of the things Mao and his co-leaders said in the 1950s and even in the 1960s, but this was mostly rhetorical. The concept of globalization then was so different to that which exists now it is hard to make much sense of Chau's claim. China was surely more a newly-established country with vast internal challenges that was fighting for international recognition and legitimacy. That it dreamed of being a global power seems far too strong.

This links to the second issue, which is that Chau divines in Maoist China's activities in Africa a clear and well worked out strategy. This is often claimed about Chinese policy making, whether it be economic or in international affairs. The notion that the leadership in Beijing had a very specific idea of what they were doing, how they were doing it, and why, was, and remains, comforting. But the messes into which China got in Africa that Chau himself explains over this period should surely caution us against holding to this notion to strongly. Chau states it far too powerfully, and places too much of an onus on it.

That means that there are parts of his analysis that are driven by this belief in a strong Chinese strategy which at best are arguable, and at worst simply wrong. In any case, China's engagement in Africa now is far less ideologically driven, and much less informed by some grand vision of its purpose. This implies that they will be far more successful at their second attempt to dig deep roots into the continent than they were during their first, where their record was so mixed and controversial.

Exploiting Africa: The Influence of Maoist China in Algeria, Ghana, and Tanzania, Donovan C Chau (US Naval Institute Press, April 2014)

Debating China: The U.S.-China Relationship in Ten Conversations by Nina Hachigian (ed.)

reviewed by Kerry Brown

18 June 2014 — *Debating China* is a misnomer as a title. In fact, this book is very much about US-China relations, and is a debate about both. The subtitle makes this clear enough. Americans tend to regard the only relationship that really matters as being that between the rest of the world and themselves. It seems that most of the Chinese interlocutors in this book share this principle about their own country, with many repeating that the "key" relationship of the modern era is the US-China one.

For all the differences between them, in hubris and grand feeling about their nation's mission and global status, the US and China are very similar, and this comes through in many of the dialogues, where the rest of the world gets only a very brief look in, and then only as a field of operation for the two big players.

In half of the ten written dialogues in this collection, the onus is on the US presenting views of China, and the Chinese partner in the dialogue then responding. This gives the US an offensive, and the Chinese a more defensive, tone.

The superb political economist Yao Yang of Beijing University bucks this trend by actually shifting the territory onto the opponent by asking some trenchant questions about inequality and social mobility in the US to Barry Naughton. But it is clear in this exchange that even a very sophisticated intellectual who has direct experience of the US carries around some interesting preconceptions. Yao for instance implies that the very wide provision of education in the US is in many ways a disincentive as it devalues having a tertiary level degree. That would cut against most received wisdom in the West which would argue that the more you can get into higher education, the better.

In the 21st century, Yao Yang shows that it is the Chinese who are the most ingrained elitists, under the socialist system.

There are few surprises in the dialogue between Andrew Nathan and Zhou Qi on rights and values issues. Zhou Qi presents a variation of the "rights are collective, and dependent on material well-being coming first" argument, thrown back at most when they deal with the Chinese government or its apologists in this area in China at any formal level. Nathan then produces a very specific list of cases where justice and due process evidently, at least in the view of many outsiders, broke down in China—people like Liu Xiaobo, Wei Jingsheng, and Chen Guangcheng. Zhou Qi sidesteps this and then attacks US values.

The dialogue on military issues is equally entrenched, with the Christopher Twomey focusing on steep budget rises for army expenditure in China over the last few years and claims of huge Chinese activity in the cyberspace area, and Xu Hui replying that, compared to GDP, China's military spend is low, and that the origin of most cyber attacks can't be proved, so why all the finger pointing?

In other areas, however, there is little space for real disagreement. Energy and the environment, media, global development and investment see more convergence than dissent. On the latter, Elizabeth Economy and Zha Daojiang map out some areas where Chinese and American companies might be able to cooperate much more in Africa and other developing areas by pooling their relative strengths now—for Chinese companies, capital and capacity, and for US ones expertise and local knowledge.

Needless to say, the Taiwan and Tibet issues (though the latter only somewhat peripherally) show the greatest differences over specific issues of policy, with Allan Romberg arguing clearly that Taiwan is only likely to be a resolvable issue when both sides have changed profoundly in the decades ahead, and Jia Qingguo showing a staggering, perhaps deliberate, ignorance of public sentiment on the island and simply stating that in their hearts, all Taiwanese wish to be reunited with the motherland, if only the US would get out of the way.

There is one word that crops up throughout the different dialogues, with the variations in theme and tone and treatment, and that is "trust". This is very puzzling. The US and China seem convinced they need to trust each other, and Wang Jisi and Kenneth Lieberthal in the opening dialogue state that it is strange after so much interaction and talk that the US and China trust each other less now than they did maybe 25 years ago, before Tiananmen.

Why knowing more about a partner should necessarily mean you trust them seems a big assumption. Often, the more one knows, the more space there is for doubt and questioning about an opponent. Knowledge can aid trust, but also breed distrust. There is no reason why China and the US should trust, because they are in many ways very different partners, and as the dialogues in this book illustrate, their mindsets are contrasting.

The most successful of the dialogues illustrate how best to handle this, with concessions to some of the opponent's views, but no shirking away from the clear differences that still lie between the two sides.

The one conclusion that one comes away from reading this book is that Americans and Chinese do have a profoundly different view of how the world should be, perhaps more so than they are ever that willing to clearly state. This is a collection of people on each side with a lifetime of engagement, experience and understanding of each other.

It would be interesting to put figures from China and the US without this next to each other—say an executive of a Chinese company operating in Africa, and one from a US company competing with them there. That would be a much more edgy and complex debate, and it is to that sort of space that the discussion needs to finally reach.

Debating China: The U.S.-China Relationship in Ten Conversations, Nina Hachigian (Editor) (Oxford University Press, USA, January 2014)

THE CHINESE
LABOUR CORPS

MARK O'NEILL

The Chinese Labour Corps: The Forgotten Chinese Labourers of the First World War by Mark O'Neill

reviewed by Juan José Morales

15 June 2014 — The 100th anniversary of the First World War has prompted the publication of books that continue to shed light on the conflict, an upheaval whose consequences are still apparent today. The Great War had a significant influence in the development of modern China, shaping her attitudes toward her own sovereignty and her foreign relations in ways that still profoundly reverberate.

When war broke out in Europe in 1914, China was emerging from millennia of dynastic rule that had ended in 1911 after the Xinhai Revolution, mired in political instability, warlordism and semi-feudal social and economic structures. The fragility of the newly-born republic was compounded by *de facto* colonial impositions: there were twenty-seven foreign concessions in Chinese soil where the Chinese government had no jurisdiction, while its economy was crippled by the huge indemnities imposed after the Boxer Rebellion. The situation became even more critical when in November 1914 Japan seized the German concessions in Shandong, a region of great strategic importance, with the acquiescence of the European powers, action that China had to witness helplessly.

In an attempt to alleviate those humiliating conditions, the Chinese government offered to aid the Allies with a contingent of laborers to be recruited by their representatives in China. Thousands left to support the Allies in Europe, by far the largest contingent of foreign workers to serve in the War.

Mark O'Neill, an author and journalist who has reported on China for more than three decades, brings these men to the history's forefront. He benefits from his research on the records left by his grandfather, Rev. Frederick O'Neill, an Irish Presbyterian missionary who had lived in China since 1897 and who served in the Chinese general hospital at Noyelles-sur-Mer. The author also draws on the few scholarly monographs on the Chinese laborers published recently by Xuo Guoqi, Li Ma, Brian Fawcett and Gregory James. O'Neill succinctly describes the circumstances that led to the workers' engagement, who they were, why they went, what they did and what happened to them afterwards.

The Chinese diplomatic efforts were led by Liang Shiyi. The French accepted the offer in June 1915, with whom Liang managed to negotiate basic rights and relatively favorable conditions for the workers. He had less success with the British, who accepted a year later—not coincidentally—during the Battle of the Somme.

Most of the workers came from North China, mainly from Shandong; the majority were illiterate and of very humble background. O'Neill begins with a letter by one of the few men whose name is known, Yuan Chun, and then recounts the relevant facts:

> Yuan was one of some 135,000 Chinese men who were sent to France and Belgium between 1916 and 1922 to help the Allied war effort. They loaded cargoes, dug trenches, filled sandbags, repaired tanks and artillery; they laid railway lines, repaired roads, built ports and aerodromes; they removed animal carcasses and ammunition from the battlefield, collected the bodies of the dead and built the graves to bury them... 94,400 men worked for the British Army... 40,000 worked for France. Of this number, around 10,000 were 'lent' to help the American Expeditionary Forces... Around 3,000 of the workers died from injuries during bombing and shelling [and other causes]. At least 700 men died in German submarine attacks before they have even set foot in Europe.

Mistreatment and discrimination by the officers and the people of the countries these men were helping were unfortunately all too common. In protest against their working conditions, the laborers had to resort to strikes and mutinies, sometimes violently repressed.

One major difficulty was the acute shortage of translators, but there were institutions to support these workers too, like the YMCA and the WSM (Work Study Movement). There they celebrated Chinese festivals and received some education; volunteers also wrote letters for them, "as many as 50,000 letters a month were sent from France to China."

Among those volunteers were bright young Chinese of privileged backgrounds and from scholarly families, men like Li Shizeng, James Yen or philosopher Lin Yu-tang. China's social classes had lived completely apart from one another—a deep fracture that the writer Lu Xun had denounced as an obstacle to Chinese progress—but away from home they were to discover each other, and as O'Neill acknowledges, "The impact was greater on the Chinese intellectuals who engaged with the workers" than the other way around.

After the armistice, the Chinese laborers carried on the tasks of reconstruction until their contracts finished. Then, all those who served under the British had to return home. Those working for the French were allowed to stay: about 3,000 remained in France—years later some of those Shandong men crossed the border to join the International Brigades during the Spanish Civil War.

The memories of these men fell soon into obscurity even though their accomplishments were highly praised in their own day by the leaders of the nations they served. Marshall Foch said:

> They were first-class workers who could be made into excellent soldiers, capable for exemplary bearing under modern artillery fire.

For the first time in modern history China had engaged in foreign affairs outside the country. The Chinese laborers' contribution gained China a place at the victors' parade and at the negotiating table at the Treaty of Versailles—although not on an equal footing and the Chinese representatives did not sign it.

However, the laborers' participation did not achieve any purpose: nothing changed. The Chinese people's aspirations were betrayed both by the Chinese government and the Western powers who maintained their own privileges in China and allowed Japan to retain the Shandong concessions; the Boxer indemnities continued to be paid until 1940.

This outrageous outcome sparked student demonstrations in Beijing on 4 May 1919, leading to what is known as May 4th Movement, entrenching the mistrust of Western powers as duplicitous, setting the country in search for its own path of modernization and in pursuit of a new national identity.

The Chinese Labour Corps: The Forgotten Chinese Labourers of the First World War, Mark O'Neill (Penguin China, March 2014)

The Forbidden Game: Golf and the Chinese Dream by Dan Washburn

reviewed by John D. Van Fleet

11 June 2014 — In 1937, Carl Crow, by then a 25-year veteran of Shanghai, published *400 Million Customers*, a work that remains one of the most nuanced and perceptive looks at the Chinese consumer and business environment ever printed. In the middle of the last decade, Tom Doctoroff echoed Crow with his *Billions* (2005), and James McGregor did so more directly with *One Billion Customers* (2006). The more recent books align with the original not only in title—they also seek to illuminate the China business environment, to the benefit of foreigners seeking success, or trying to avoid failure, in the Middle Kingdom.

China has nowhere near 400 million golfers, but it has at least tens of millions, and the number is growing rapidly. But most play on courses that are technically illegal, because Beijing has had a general moratorium on golf course building for decades. And by definition China's golfers are among the wealthiest citizens of the PRC—a typical round of golf in one of the Shanghai suburbs costs nearly RMB1,000 (US$160), about half the monthly minimum wage in the city.

So one might not immediately expect this story of golf in China to be anything more than a description of tawdry local corruption and the *nouveau riche*. (The Chinese term for these folks, 土豪, *tuhao*, literally "the brave of the dirt", carries all the negative connotation that the borrowed-from-French term does in English, and of the Japanese *narikin* (成金), "become money", closer to the European insult. There is no class of "old rich" in mainland China, as the victorious Communist Party reduced all of those families to penury or worse starting in the 1940s.)

But that expectation is wrong. Dan Washburn's *The Forbidden Game* pleasantly surprises on a few levels. First, he's crafted a tale not only of the development of golf in China, but of the development of post-Mao China overall, centered on three individuals: one of China's first professional golfers, Zhou Xunshu, originally from one of China's poorest provinces; Martin Moore, perhaps China's most famous builder of golf courses; and villager Wang, a peasant farmer whose life is completely transformed when his land is essentially stolen by corrupt local officials and leased to the mega-rich Chu family of Hong Kong for the creation of Mission Hills Hainan. (Hainan, an island just offshore from Guangdong Province, is often referred to, with more optimism than precision, as China's Hawaii.)

Second, the convoluted, legally-challenged and sometimes counter-intuitive development of golf in China proves an excellent window into China's overall development during the past three decades, precisely because China's overall development has been convoluted, legally murky and often counter-intuitive.

The Communist Party of China officially considers golf a bourgeois pastime—Washburn describes how government officials use false names when they play, and wear long-sleeve shirts so that they don't get the golfer's tan, from mid-bicep down. Washburn has said elsewhere that

> Golf is a symbol of corruption, rural land rights disputes, environmental neglect, the growing gap between rich and poor, and a shrinking supply of arable land. In many ways golf, and the complex world that surrounds it in China, is a microcosm of the contradictory country as a whole.

Author James Fallows, writing elsewhere, captured the point in fewer words, describing *The Forbidden Game* as "another valuable 'universal in the particular' story of China." So the book stands proudly on the shelf (or in the Kindle folder) next to Crow's 1937 work and others that foster greater understanding of China.

Mission Hills Hainan has become the second-largest golf course development in the world, behind Mission Hills Shenzhen, in China's southern Guangdong Province—both projects of the Chu family, whose members feature prominently in Washburn's work. Washburn's telling of the story abounds in bribery, collusion and other nefarious behavior. Washburn spent hundreds of hours bird-dogging Zhou through the latter's trials and tribulations as he became a fully professional golfer, and describes how Zhou taught himself to play, in the early days using broken clubs that he'd tape together. Washburn's evocation of his visits to Zhou's hometown, Qixin, are alone worth the price of his book. His obvious intimacy with the culture and language infuse and strengthen the work.

The Forbidden Game is a highly interesting tale, sometimes not so well told. The work reads like an assembly of previous articles and such, so is marred by repetition—the reader needs to be told once or twice, not a dozen times, that golf courses are technically illegal in China, that corrupt local officials make money by doing deals with developers at the expense of local residents, etc. These carpentry errors and some outright grammatical misses indicate the need for a better editor.

But those are construction problems; the foundation remains solid. *The Forbidden Game* is well worth reading.

The Forbidden Game: Golf and the Chinese Dream, Dan Washburn (ONEWorld Publications, July 2014)

Asia's Cauldron: The South China Sea and the End of a Stable Pacific by Robert D. Kaplan

reviewed by Peter Gordon

7 June 2014 — Headlines from the past few days include "Chuck Hagel: Beijing 'destabilising' South China Sea" (BBC), "Xi says China won't stir trouble in South China Sea" (Reuters), "Template for the South China Sea" (New York Times editorial), "China Can Sink All the Boats in the South China Sea" (Salon), and that's just first inch or so of Google News.

Robert D. Kaplan's new book *Asia's Cauldron: The South China Sea and the End of a Stable Pacific* therefore seems timely indeed. Kaplan, reprising a theme from his *The Revenge of Geography*, explains why, for reasons of geography, the South China Sea is pivotal. He also notes (again reprising a theme from his older book *Monsoon*) the importance of the Indian Ocean and that the South China Sea is where the Indian and Pacific Oceans meet: the French had it right, he says, when they named the region Indochina.

Asia's Cauldron would serve well as a briefing document for those who don't keep up with the newspapers and other relevant publications on a regular basis. Kaplan runs through the region country by country, providing a brief history of each, segueing to the military capabilities, current politics and international relations. Rather than tables of data, the relatively slim volume is instead littered with quotes gleaned from various interviews and personal observations of everything from the ruins of Vietnam's Indian-inspired Champa kingdom to street scenes in contemporary Manila. Kaplan's prose is easy and accessible; this is not a taxing read.

Kaplan is not entirely unsympathetic to Chinese perspectives. A particularly illuminating theme of the book is the comparison to the Caribbean:

> Like the Caribbean, punctuated as it is by small island states and enveloped by a continent-sized United States, the South China Sea is an obvious arena for the projection of power by a continent-sized nation, which also to a significant extent envelopes it.

Kaplan's overall argument is one that will come as no surprise to anyone wont to click on the sorts of headlines listed above: the South China Sea, he argues, is an area of contention; China's ambitions in the region are supported by an increasing economic and military presence; the other countries are resisting and intend to resist further; and the United States's ability to maintain a *pax Americana* is waning.

The opposite of stability is not necessarily armed conflict; Kaplan does not argue that the latter is inevitable, rather that the situation is likely to get messier:

> a nervous world, crowded with warships and oil tankers, one of incessant war games and without necessarily leading to actual combat... The age of simple American dominance, as it existed through all of the Cold War decades and immediately beyond, will likely have to pass. A more anxious, complicated world awaits us.

Those who think otherwise, either that China's South Sea claims are indisputable and will inherently prevail or that the United States can—or even attempt to—continue to maintain the *status quo ante*, had best read this book.

Asia's Cauldron nevertheless contains passages that a judicious writer or his editor might have removed. Musing on Singapore's skyline, Kaplan writes:

> At work was the abstract genius of the Chinese, who understand the conceptual utility of empty spaces; as opposed to the Indianized Malay mind, which is more at home in the world of thickly colored and deliciously cluttered textiles, with their floral and cartouche patterns...

Or on the Philippines:

> ... despite what the guidebooks claim, there really isn't any distinctive Filipino cuisine beyond fish, pork and indifferently cooked rice.

Regardless of what one thinks of statements like these, they are tangential to the discussion at hand. Nor are these throw-away lines restricted to cuisine and psychological generalization: the chapter on Taiwan concludes that "Chiang Kai-shek may yet turn out to be a more important historical figure than Mao Zedong."

Those who are *au courant* with Asia geopolitics might well be able to make do with Kaplan's conclusions, which he has outlined in several essays elsewhere. Those less familiar will find this, the off-subject editorial asides notwithstanding, a clear and reasonably open-minded introduction to a part of the world that is already contentious and almost certain to remain so.

Asia's Cauldron: The South China Sea and the End of a Stable Pacific, Robert D Kaplan (Random House, March 2014)

Baijiu: The Essential Guide to Chinese Spirits by Derek Sandhaus

reviewed by Jonathan Chatwin

31 May 2014 — The first few months of living in China can be regarded as a series of rites of passage, most of which, once overcome, are viewed as proud markers of one's increasing integration into Chinese culture. Those who have not yet faced down the more particular aspects of life in the Middle Kingdom ("You've really never eaten locusts/snake/chicken feet/ Chongqing hot pot?" etc.) tend to be viewed as dilettantes and treated correspondingly.

However, even for those who have ticked off the years, provinces and mysterious foodstuffs, there generally remains an obstacle to the development of a sense of true integration: baijiu, China's national spirit. The challenge it poses results from its ubiquity: baijiu, a clear spirit which often exceeds 50% in alcohol content, is at the heart of Chinese social and dining culture, fulfilling the same essential ceremonial and lubricating role at both the dimly-lit local restaurant and the lavish banquet hall.

Unlike other rites of passage, the drinking of baijiu cannot just be endured once or twice and forgotten about; it confronts one at every turn. Conceptually, this shouldn't be a problem for expats, who generally pride themselves on their capacity for alcohol consumption. However (and at the risk of encouraging a slew of correspondence from old China hands claiming to love the stuff), I know not a single Westerner who professes to enjoy drinking baijiu.

Apart, that is, from Derek Sandhaus, whose new book, *Baijiu: The Essential Guide to Chinese Spirits*, is part reference book, and part evangelical entreaty. After half a decade of living in China and doing his best to avoid baijiu, Sandhaus decided in 2011 that the time had come to overcome his distaste for it.

He embarked on a Gladwellian project, documented on his blog, in which, over six months or so, he drank his way through 300 shots of baijiu—the threshold, it is claimed, at which the spirit becomes palatable. Sandhaus arrived at the other side of this endeavor having not just acquired a tolerance for baijiu, but an actual affection for the spirit.

Hence the dual personality of the book that emerged from his project; Sandhaus wants not only to educate the reader on the history and production of baijiu, but also to persuade the world to appreciate and take seriously what is, astonishingly, the best selling strong alcohol in the world.

The book is split into two sections. In the first, the author outlines the history and manufacturing process of baijiu. Emphasising the fact that "baijiu" is an umbrella term which applies to a range of spirits "that can be as dissimilar from one another as tequila and rum," Sandhaus walks the reader through the evolution of the spirit, and the various unique methods of production.

For those who assume the process to be somewhat unsophisticated, this section offers a correction; though ancient in its principles, the production of baijiu is equally as complex and refined as that of, say, single malt Scotch. The key distinction of the process is that, unlike Western spirits, the grains used to produce baijiu (predominantly sorghum and rice) are fermented in a solid state: the grains are crushed and moistened, and kept in a warm, dark environment until natural yeasts and bacteria develop. The resulting product, known as *qu*, is then ground and steamed in a pot still to produce the distillate that will, after careful ageing in clay pots, become baijiu.

The second section of the book provides useful context and tasting notes for various brands of baijiu, ranging from the "drink of the Chinese everyman", and downfall of many a Western visitor, Hongxing Erguotou, through to the notorious Kweichow Moutai, traditional fuel of the communist party (though now suffering a high-profile drop in sales, following Xi Jinping's anti-corruption crackdown).

Baijiu: The Essential Guide to Chinese Spirits fulfils its primary educational role admirably; scrupulously researched and systematically laid out, this slim volume does an excellent job of demystifying baijiu.

However, as the reaction of generations of expats in China has established, convincing the world to take Chinese spirits seriously will be something of a bigger job, and only time will tell whether baijiu will rise to take its place behind the cocktail bars of London and New York.

Engendering cultural adoption of the foreign or new is somewhat akin to the process of urban gentrification; it takes a few enthusiastic outliers to kickstart the process and overturn prejudices, but, before you know it, the irredeemable has become the mainstream. It's happened before: viz. Brooklyn/East London/espresso/foie gras/scotch whisky. Why shouldn't baijiu be next?

Baijiu: The Essential Guide to Chinese Spirits, Derek Sandhaus (Penguin China, May 2014)

Green Politics in China: Environmental Governance and State-Society Relations by Joy Y. Zhang and Michael Barr

reviewed by Coraline Goron

21 May 2014 — Hidden behind the somewhat academic title of *Green Politics in China: Environmental Governance and State-Society Relations* is a valuable depiction of China's nascent grassroots civil society. Whereas the bulk of recent studies on similar topics have focused on the evolving nature of the authoritarian regime, this book's originality stems from its analysis of state-society relations from a "bottom-up" perspective. The grassroots narrative they persuasively develop is grounded in both large volumes of Chinese-language scholarly and popular works and extensive field-work including 32 interviews with representatives from 14 organizations across China (though admittedly most are from Beijing-based Environmental NGOs).

The authors defend the idea that contrary to much mainstream opinion, Chinese grassroots ENGOs (environmental non-government organizations) are not the weak and submissive organizations they are normally portrayed as being, although the dominance of the State is never in question. Instead the "conformist rebels"—as the authors call them—running them have found creative strategies to push the boundaries of public participation in the non-democratic political process and in doing so have managed to initiate a positive dynamic promoting the "green" agenda among Chinese society. The authors thereby contribute to the movement in China studies that is unsatisfied with the prevalent view of a State vs Society dichotomy.[1]

The structure of the book reflects this bottom-up approach. Using the lens of these activists' views and perceptions, the authors convey a complex picture of how Chinese grassroots society is struggling to cope with deep and rapid change while pursuing the sometimes conflicting aspirations of prosperity and stability, social justice and a more accountable administration.

The authors rightly highlight the often overlooked societal barriers to green policies in developing countries, stemming from the failure to perceive the extent of environmental degradation and the higher public tolerance of such harm as a price willingly paid for rising prosperity. Illustrative is the anecdote in the book with a peasant observing the smoke bellowing out of the local factory's chimneys saying

> "See that white smoke? It is like we are manufacturing clouds in the sky. That is a pretty scene. We are proud of it!"

The West's demands for China to raise its environmental standards were long perceived as self-serving, hypocritical and imperialist. Chinese books with titles like *Low Carbon Plot: China's vital war with the US and Europe* (Gou, 2010) are evidence that such arguments still find popular support.

These views are common in the developing world and hardly unique to China. But here, with the communist legacy absolving individuals from the responsibility for the provision and protection of public goods, they are an additional impediment to NGOs mobilization efforts.

Against this background, the authors re-evaluate Chinese ENGOs' outreach and educational activities, which have often been casually dismissed as "strategies of the weak" in comparison with the more vocal advocacy campaigns in the West. The authors show why Chinese ENGOs feel they must, in spite of the difficulties, actively and durably mobilize citizens to their side. One NGO leader laments:

> "City dwellers, especially the young generation [...] do not have any bond with nature. If you suggest we should cut down the tree to make paper, they'd say so what, go ahead..."

* * *

The political constraints on NGOs' activities in China, spanning the struggle for legal status, fighting censorship and secrecy to obtain information and withstanding pressure not to challenge the authority of the state, are a constant factor in the day-to-day operation of Chinese ENGOs.

But the authors show that even within these constraints there is space left for creative and effective strategies. Most "underground" ENGOs (either not registered at all or registered in other categories like companies) operate "over-ground" without obstruction from the Party, even though, being unofficial, they are admittedly even more vulnerable to policy reversal and corruption. But the authors argue that Chinese ENGOs have nonetheless succeeded in achieving an unprecedented—albeit limited—realignment of power relations between the State and civil society and that, paradoxically, this very cooperation and engagement with the State fosters their legitimacy and credibility in the eyes of the wider public.[2]

The diversity of strategies pursued by Chinese ENGOs is illustrated with a series of case studies and do include advocacy. One, for example, shows the success of "I Monitor the Air for My Country", campaign which skillfully played on the independent monitoring published by the US Embassy in Beijing, and which forced its way into the revision of the Chinese Air Quality Standard in 2012. A "state secret" not included in the first draft of the regulation, "PM 2.5" (micro-air particles of less than 2.5μm diameter that are particularly health-damaging) became a "buzz word" in the space of weeks. The mobilization success of the environmentalists resulted not only in the upgrading of the standard, but also speeded the installation of public air quality monitoring machines throughout the country and allowed studies on the health consequences of air pollution to be shared publicly with the blessing of public authorities (for instance, *Dangerous Breathing*, co-produced in 2012 by Greenpeace China and Peking University).

And in the apocalyptic air pollution winter of 2013, state-owned oil producers faced public outrage, which led government to demand higher-quality diesel fuel. Overall, these cases significantly revise the traditional view of China's state-society relations as merely a story of repression and control. The authors' presentation is made all the more effective thanks to the attention to detail and bottom-up perspectives applied.

The authors largely restrict their conclusions about the nature of the Chinese State to those than can be drawn directly from their empirical investigations. As something of a consequence, their discussion of China's "fragmented" authoritarian environmentalism in the last chapter (a concept describing the conflicting lines of authority within the Party/State's administration, notably between Beijing and provincial and local governments) seems incomplete. In particular, the link between their suggested model and state-society relations remains unexplained. There is on the other hand a lengthy and some tangential description of the Government's green agenda under the banner of "ecological civilization" (生态文明 *shengtai wenming*, a concept coined by former President Hu Jintao at the 17th Party Congress in 2007 and then given full constitutional status at the 18th Party Congress in December 2012).

The authors also do not address the parallel phenomenon of environmental protests movements which can be seen, by contrast, as the openly confrontational face of green activism in China. In recent years, the number of environmental-led mass incidents has risen exponentially.[3] Many have received wide media coverage, such as the events in Xiamen in 2008, in Dalian in 2009, in Shifan in 2012, Qidong and Ningbo in 2012.

A comprehensive picture of the societal landscape of green activism "with Chinese characteristics" arguably requires attention to both political dynamics and explore the relation between the two. An examination of the confrontation of these parallel courses of "green activism" could lead to a more comprehensive understanding of the complex power dynamics at play in the triangle between "social movements", "organized civil society" and the state in China.

Green Politics in China does not, therefore, tell the entire story. But it nevertheless provides a good introduction to a crucial aspect of environmental policy-making and implementation in China as well a good counter-example to the monolithic model of Chinese politics.

Notes:
[1] see e.g. Ho and Edmonds' *China's Embedded Activism* (2008) and *Shapiro's China's Environmental Challenges*, 2012, both discussed here.
[2] Public support and volunteering are a very substantial resource for Chinese grassroots NGOs, as shown by Spires et al, "Societal Support for China's Grass-Roots NGOs" (2014)
[3] See e.g. Johnson, "Environmentalism and NIMBYism in China" (2010)

Green Politics in China; Environmental Governance and State-society Relations, Joy Y Zhang, Michael D Barr (Pluto Press, June 2013)

China's Second Continent: How a Million Migrants are Building a New Empire in Africa by Howard French

reviewed by Kerry Brown

16 May 2014 — The story of China in Africa has attracted considerable attention over the last few years, particularly around the time of the Beijing Olympics in 2008. Many will remember such august figures as Mia Farrow and Stephen Spielberg condemning China over its role in Sudan and the civil war there, claiming that it had supplied arms to the government to suppress opponents, with some even claiming its complicity in genocide.

China learned the hard way that Africa is a hard place to work in. But as Howard French, a journalist of rich experience in both Africa and China makes clear in his new account, *China's Second Continent: How a Million Migrants are Building a New Empire in Africa*, this is a mixed story. For those that condemn China's role in the world's poorest continent, French finds plenty of evidence that Beijing's aid money, its funding for infrastructure and its trade links are making a difference. They might sometimes be messy and chaotic, but they are delivering wealth and better living standards to many people who have largely been unreached by western business and charity links.

The great contribution that French makes is to give a human face and narrative to a story that has until now been largely abstract. There have been good and detailed studies of China's emerging economic and geopolitical role in Africa over the last decade, but it has been hard to hear the voices of the individuals involved.

French's excellent journalist training is much in evidence. He gives this story voices, conveyed directly, as he also makes clear his own position as he listens to them.

The Chinese he engages with across the countries he travels through often betray condescension towards locals. One businessman from southern China, despite relocating over a decade before, complains about how Africans only like dancing and don't know how to work hard. Others defend the high use of Chinese imported labor because of the unreliability of African workers.

Not that the Chinese attitudes towards their homeland are any easier on life there. Many explain their coming to a harsh, new and challenging environment as worthwhile because of the escape route it gives from a country ruled by bullying and predatory local officials. At least in Africa, their money gives them clout and influence. One migrant puts it pithily: you can own land in Africa. In China, it always belongs to the government, and they can take it away from you and reduce you to poverty at will.

French raises a number of interesting angles. Resources matter in the Chinese adventure in Africa, but in the longer term it will probably be the emerging market for Chinese manufactured goods that will be more important—that, and the abundance of unexploited arable land which is of such interest to a China that has largely despoiled or built on its own farmland.

Nor is there much credibility in the idea of some grand state strategy run from Beijing. The evidence French finds is of a continent being economically conquered by hundreds of thousands of Chinese coming for different reasons, chasing different dreams, and with very little relationship with the government and ruling party of the land they have left. Many complain that the Chinese state, far from helping in their business conquest of Africa, acts as a brake and impediment, taking steps they believe far too modest and cautious in a place where opportunity is everywhere.

And for Africans, long figured as passive agents in all of this new activity, French has a prescient warning. Chinese activity is morally neutral. It can do great good, but, for those naïve or unskilled in dealing with it, it can also do harm. Elites can grow corrupt and venal on the wealth China is bringing, and allow their countries to grow vulnerable and be easy to exploit.

For a country that also has its own searing experience of what it means to be bullied and victimized, China has a harder and more defined self-interest in how it behaves in a place like Africa now. It says it seeks win-win outcomes, but at the end of the day it is prosecuting activity for the prosperity and benefit of China.

Africans that can find ways to work in this narrative that strengthens them are on to a winning patch. And the need for unity in their response to the new interests of China across the 54 states of Africa is important, just as it is in Europe where individual countries have little weight when they bargain with the vast Chinese market now, but matter when they work together.

The need to create an African consensus on what the opportunities and risks are that come from China's keen interest in their continent is now critical. And French's book gives the best diagnostic of where the negatives and positives lie that currently exists on this subject.

China's Second Continent: How a Million Migrants Are Building a New Empire in Africa, Howard W French (Knopf Publishing Group, May 2014)

Junkyard Planet: Travels in the Billion-Dollar Trash Trade by Adam Minter

reviewed by Bill Purves

9 May 2014 — His wife says it best: "I never knew garbage until I knew Adam Minter."

Minter spent his high school days working in the family scrap yard in the US, but these days he reports from Shanghai for Bloomberg, freelancing on the side for publications like Scrap and Recycling International.

After reading *Junkyard Planet* you'll have to agree: Minter certainly knows his scrap.

The planetary junkyard is a multifarious and complicated place.

A bum scavenges beverage cans out of trash bins and sells them to a roving scrap buyer with a pickup truck. The buyer sells the paper and metals he collects to a local scrap yard which acts as an accumulator, selling on bales of newspapers, cans, wire and used plumbing to larger yards that specialize.

Those larger yards sell container loads to buyers from China who ship the containers to Shenzhen for sorting and processing. Once the insulation has been stripped from the wire and the shredded washing machine motors have been sorted (by hand) into their copper, white metal and aluminum components, the pure metal is sold on to foundries which do the actual recycling—turning used metal or paper into new ingots or cardboard.

Why China? The immediate assumption is about cheap labor, but if labor costs were the key it would all be done in Bangladesh or Burkina Faso.

China is a scrap magnet because of all the stuff it sells to the US It's all shipped in containers. The US sells few manufactured goods to China, so most of the containers have to be shipped back empty. Sending a container load from Los Angeles to Shenzhen might cost US$400, from Los Angeles to Chicago might cost $2400. When you're moving scrap around, shipping costs make all the difference. So China gets inexpensive raw materials.

But an even more important point is that today the US doesn't manufacture enough to recycle all the scrap metal it throws away.

This is a complicated tale. In *Junkyard Planet* it's told as a travelogue. Minter describes in the first person visiting scrap yards, processing facilities and foundries with some of the many colorful characters at the heart of the scrap trade.

His account focuses mostly on China ("the capital of the junkyard planet") and the US ("the Saudi Arabia of scrap") but he detours briefly to Europe and Malaysia and to some truly godforsaken junk yards in India.

He has plenty to choose from. The industry's long, worldwide supply chain turns over $500 billion a year and employs more people than any other business apart from agriculture.

Minter also makes the case as an environmentalist. He sorts his trash and fully subscribes to "reduce, reuse, recycle"; though "reduce" doesn't get much of a look-in during his account of his travels.

Your 2G phone is no longer in demand even in Africa, but don't just chuck it in with the food scraps and lawn clippings. There are workers in China who specialize in extracting the chips and firms who recycle them into talking dolls and other gadgets. The copper, zinc and precious metals are reclaimed from the circuit board, and the plastic is shredded and remelted.

If your drink cans didn't go to China they would end up as landfill, and recycling a ton of aluminum uses about 8% of the energy required to smelt it from newly mined alumina and bauxite. Minter makes a convincing case.

His Bloomberg journalistic standards in evidence, Minter has turned out a book with a detailed, useful index and quite a few interesting and relevant photographs. His account contains enough statistics to qualify as a casual reference, but they don't get in the way of the human stories it tells.

Liquids (used solvents, chemical plant by-products, used plating solution, etc.) aren't mentioned (Minter describes himself as metal-centric), but otherwise the book provides a useful tour of today's junkyard planet.

Minter will convince you, as he has his wife, that it's a topic worthy of being much more widely understood.

Junkyard Planet: Travels in the Billion-Dollar Trash Trade, Adam Minter (Bloomsbury Publishing PLC, November 2013)

Mr. Selden's Map of China: Decoding the Secrets of a Vanished Cartographer by Timothy Brook

reviewed by Tim O'Connell

4 May 2014 — What turned out to be the most important Chinese map of the past seven hundred years had been gathering dust in the basement stacks of Oxford's Bodleian Library for nearly a century, when in 2008 an American historian became curious about an old catalogue listing and called it up. Records showed that the one-by-two-meter scroll, beautifully drawn and colored in the style of a Chinese landscape painting, arrived at the Bodleian in 1659 as part of a large bequest of books and manuscripts by the late John Selden, the foremost English legal scholar of his time, and a prime architect of the international law of the sea.

Intriguingly highlighted in Selden's will as having been "taken ... by an englishe comander who being pressed exceedingly to restore it at good ransome would not parte with it," the late Ming-era map broke with all Chinese cartographical convention by shunting the Celestial Empire into a corner and focusing on the South China Sea. There the ocean's greenish wash of billowy waves is criss-crossed with what are clearly eighteen ruler-straight trading routes connecting the major ports of the region, from Japan in the north to the Philippines, Southeast Asia and the Spice Islands in the south, the first sea chart in history to do so on this scale. Who had created this unique, beautiful and mysterious work of art, for what purpose, and how had it come to rest in Stuart England?

Timothy Brook, a distinguished Professor of History at the University of British Columbia and authority on Ming China, tackles that puzzle in his fascinating new book, *Mr. Selden's Map of China: Decoding the Secrets of a Vanished Cartographer.* His earlier award-winning bestseller, *Vermeer's Hat: The Seventeenth Century and the Dawn of the Global World,* uses the items depicted in the tableaux of the Dutch painter as jumping off points for a tour of the first great age of global trade, a revolutionary period of cargo, corporatism and empire that shaped the world we inhabit today. His new book employs the Selden Map in much the same way:

> It was an age of remarkable creativity and change. New vistas were opening, old horizons faltering, accepted truths giving way to controversial new ideas ... In the end, this book is not really about a map. It is about the people whose stories intersected with it. The venture succeeds if I can demonstrate how rich, how complicated and how globally networked this era was.

* * *

Mr. *Selden's Map* is as much about 17*th*-century England as late Ming China. The author works backwards in a "circling maze" from the masques of Ben Jonson and food fights at the court of James II, to the contested seas of East Asia, where the upstart East India Company and its Dutch counterpart challenged the Spanish and Portuguese for control of the lucrative spice trade. The story moves on to Fujian's dynamic seafarers and "the chimera of China trade," Ming cartography and the fascinating intricacies of navigation and chart making.

This is one of those books that humbles the general reader with the realization of just how much interesting history there is to learn—even Brook expresses astonishment at how remarkably diverse the individuals and subjects that intersect his story turn out to be:

> Odd as this may seem, one book is not enough to open all the doors hidden in the details of the map ... Those I have been able to enter have disclosed a mad variety of events and personalities that I never expected to encounter when I first looked at the map. They include the burning of Japanese erotica in London, the trade policies of Emperor Wanli, the design of the Chinese compass, Samuel Taylor Coleridge's intentional misspelling of Xanadu, the donation of human remains to the Bodleian Library, and the ancestral church of the Knights Templar, to mention but a few.

Among those personalities is the Jesuit novice Michael Shen Fuzong, converted son of a Nanjing doctor, who sailed to Europe in the 1680s and charmed the crowned heads of Europe (Louis XIV invited him back just to watch him use chopsticks, *plus ça change*). The first recorded Chinese to visit England, he worked closely with the Keeper of the Bodleian, Thomas Hyde, cataloguing collections and helping decipher the Selden Map (no Englishman could yet read Chinese)—their "ghostly translations and annotations in spidery European letters" are still visible. Hyde never learned that his exotic young friend perished off Madagascar on the return voyage.

Shen finds a modern counterpart in the scholar Xiang Da, who travelled to Oxford in 1935 on a similar cataloguing mission and later annotated the Laud Rutter (*Shun Feng Xiang Song*), another unique maritime manuscript donated to the Bodleian in 1639 that may describe the famous voyages of the early Ming navigator Zheng He (1371-1433). Xiang met an even sadder fate, tortured to death during the Cultural Revolution for his foreign travels and friendships, but not before making a calculation that may be critical to understanding the Selden Map. In a work that embodies the excitement and joys of scholarship, Brook writes:

> I like the fact that Xiang's careful work on the rutter has now come back to prove something about a map he never had the chance to see: that the ruler is indeed the scale by which the cartographer drew the routes on the Selden map. His reputation outlives his tormentors. The vindication is a small one, but among the people I hang out with, this triumph matters. Xiang was one of our finest, and this is what we do.

* * *

An engaging narrative supplemented with 16 pages of color illustrations, *Mr. Selden's Map of China* will keep any reader who enjoys a good historical detective story eagerly turning the pages. Consequently, it seems churlish to reveal too many of the author's painstakingly teased-out solutions to the codes and puzzles of this singular chart. I will confirm that Brook concludes that the panicked, debt-ridden Chinese merchant who reluctantly surrendered the scroll to the "englishe comander" probably did so in the Javan trading center of Bantam.

But in signs of a lively emerging debate, Robert Batchelor, the American scholar who first spotted the map, sees evidence in its northern portions for an origin there, perhaps in the Japanese port of Hirado, where the great China Captain Li Dan set in motion a chain of events that led indirectly to a Chinese Taiwan.

Whether Selden's long-forgotten map has anything to say about certain contested archipelagos, if it might in any way prove a "winning card in the diplomatic game China plays with its neighbors," remains for the reader to learn.

Mr. Selden's Map of China: Decoding the Secrets of a Vanished Cartographer, Timothy Brook (Bloomsbury Publishing PLC, October 2013; Profile Books, February 2014)

The Virgin Mary and Catholic Identities in Chinese History by Jeremy Clarke

reviewed by Gianni Criveller

1 May 2014 — Present-day Catholic communities in China trace their history some 400 years back, when Italian missionary Matteo Ricci initiated a mission based on friendship, cultural and scientific exchange and the preaching of Catholic faith. Visual narratives produced by Ricci and his Jesuits companions were an important component of their evangelization method, known as "accommodation", i.e. the effort of translating Catholic teaching in the Chinese context.

Many books are devoted to the Jesuit China mission, but only few of them investigate in depth how images are the most innovative characteristic of Jesuits' preaching. This book is the first, to the best of my knowledge, devoted to tracing the history and development of the visual representations of the Virgin Mary. However reducing the scope to Marian iconography only is somewhat arbitrary for the purpose of exploring the meaning and impact of Catholic iconography in China, which had in the life of Jesus its main theme (we will came back to this point).

Nevertheless, focusing on Marian iconography allows space for much new information and interpretation of this little-known aspect of Catholic life in China.

In the early 1950s, Christian relics—such as decorated stone monuments (including several tombstones) and an image of the Madonna and child (dated 1342)—were discovered in Yangzhou. These relics proved that accommodation to local style was, in the words of Dutch Sinologist Eric Zürcher, a "cultural imperative" for the acceptance of Catholicism in

China since Yuan dynasty.

The book shows how, since the early fourteenth century, images of Mary were accommodated to Chinese style: along the history, Marian iconography was inspired by what were for Catholicism unlikely models, such as the Buddhist goddess of mercy Guanyin and the Empress Dowager. The description of the complex process that lead photographs of the Empress Dowager (viewed by Catholics as a mortal enemy) to influence the portrait of Our Lady of Donglu (still the most beloved Catholic image in China) is, in my opinion, the book's most startling and innovative contribution.

From the mid-nineteenth through the early twentieth centuries, French-style images were prevalent, overshadowing Chinese Christian images. The need for a return to local style was critically felt by Chinese Catholic intellectuals and communities, realizing that they could not any longer afford to be seen as a foreign body in their own country.

From early 1930s, a new wave of Catholic images in distinctive Chinese fashion were created in Beijing (at the newly-founded Furen University) and in Shanghai. The artists resumed earlier adaptation efforts, especially by Late Ming missionaries such as João da Rocha and Giulio Aleni. In the 1920s, the Vatican envoy Celso Costantini was instrumental in promoting the so called "Chinese Christian art", overcoming the resistance of foreign Catholic leadership; before 1926, all Catholic bishops in China were foreign.

Everywhere in the world, Marian visual representations are a spontaneous channel promoting the process of inculturation. The devotion towards Mary touches emotions that are to be expressed in a congenial style, so we have Mary portrayed in different cultural and ethnic modes, as black, latin, aboriginal, white etc. Devotion to the Virgin Mary is a very distinctive (although not exclusive) characteristic of Catholicism. Through images, including Marian ones, Chinese Catholics were able to affirm their distinctive identity and find support though very difficult circumstances and tumultuous historical upheavals.

Not all Catholics feel the need to have a Chinese Madonna to enhance their devotion. The book acknowledges that the resistance, in certain Catholic quarters, to Christian images in Chinese fashion persists even today. A good example would be the mixed reactions to the painting—not mentioned in the book—of the Mother of God, Empress of China, located in the North Church in Beijing.[1] The oil painting, by a contemporary artist from Hong Kong, represents Mary and the Child looking Chinese and as wearing luxurious imperial Manchu robes. Some Beijing Catholics think that Mary, should not be artificially represented as Chinese. Chinese looks too much like Guanyin, they object. At viewing this image, I have heard Beijing Catholics saying: "We have left Buddhism. Why are we taken back there?"

There are a few minor imperfections in the book: the use of the term "Nestorians" for describing Tang dynasty missionaries from the Church of the East; 1939 Vatican document on the Rites controversy is not an apostolic letter but a simple *instruction* by Congregation for the Propagation of the Faith; and misprints, e.g. on one occasion Paul VI for Paul V.

But I find that there are a couple of significant omissions which are worth discussing in some depth. The author describes how *Illustrations of the Gospel Stories* (*Evangelicae Historiae Imagines*, 1593) by Jerónimo Nadal was the European text that served as inspiration and model for the early production of Christian iconography in China. Missionaries in China asked for a copy of the Nadal's great book of images, and it reached China before 1605. However, more words should have been spent for describing the special relationship between Jesuit worldview and images. All Jesuits were trained through the meditative methodology of visualization, known as "composition of place", initiated by the founder of the Society of Jesus, Ignatius of Loyola. This visualization is a mental creation of a space where a imaginative (in the sense of image-filled) narration takes place. The purpose was to enhance the emotional connection of the devotee with the biblical stories. The images were indispensable tools to create a meditative journey that would lead to the spiritual encounter with Jesus, the protagonist of the evangelical stories.

In the Jesuits' world, "image" was not a tool illustrating the written text. On the contrary, it was the written text which was at the service of the image. The images, acting on the receptivity of human senses, produce emotions of the heart and motions of the will. Other forms of communication, based on intellectuality, cannot produce such a personal emotional participation. The images and the illustrated books produced by the Jesuits would provide a set of visual experiences for reading and for meditation instrumental to this purpose.

Jesuit picture books in China used the ideogram *xiang* 像 to translate the term "image". In contrast to the ideogram *tu* 圖 (picture, figure), xiang indicates not only the image, but also the act of perception, and the relationship that occurs between the image and the viewer. Nicolas Standaert, who elaborated a fascinating and complex analysis on the ideogram *xiang* 像 as employed by Jesuits, affirms that the images produced by missionaries: "not only function as sacred objects of worship or meditation, but also as sacred subjects that can cause an effect."[2]

Chinese image books produced by João da Rocha (*The Method of Reciting the Rosary*, 1619) Giulio Aleni (*The Illustrated Life of the Lord of Heaven Incarnate*, 1637) and Adam Schall von Bell (we will return on the latter, as it was not mentioned in the book reviewed here) aimed at the creation of a space in which an encounter, between the divine and the devotee, might take place. Jesuit visual production in China could have been eagerly accepted by audience already familiar with similar tradition in Pure Land Buddhism.

On 8 September 1640, Adam Schall Von Bell presented the Emperor Chongzhen a beautiful and valuable illustrated book, entitled *The Life of Christ*. It was a gift from the Duke Maximilian I of Bavaria, and contained 45 images painted in miniature and was produced in a single copy, especially to be donated to the Emperor of China.

The book was brought to China by Jesuit Nicolas Trigault and probably is no longer in existence. The Jesuits, commissioning such an elaborate donation, hoped to attract the curiosity of the Emperor and to induce, if at all possible, his conversion. On that historical occasion, Adam Schall published *Images in a Booklet Presented to His Majesty*, a book that reproduced in Chinese fashion the 45 images contained in *The Life of Christ*. Several of the images include Mary, the mother of Jesus. This was the third picture book produced in China which had Nadal's *Illustrations* as model.

These points of discussion notwithstanding, *The Virgin Mary and Catholic Identities in Chinese History* offers much original information and insightful interpretations and reflections, and it makes worthwhile reading for anyone interested in Catholicism in China.

Notes

[1] Neilene Chou Wiest, "St Saviour's Madonna is looking for a cultural identity." In *South China Morning Post*, Dec. 23, 2002.

[2] Nicolas Standaert, "An Illustrated Life of Christ Presented to the Chinese Emperor". Sankt Augustin – Nettetal, 2007, p . 78.

The Virgin Mary and Catholic Identities in Chinese History, Jeremy Clarke (Hong Kong University Press, August 2013)

East Sails West: The Voyage of the Keying, 1846-1855 by Stephen Davies

reviewed by John Butler

29 April 2014 — In the ever-extending catalogue of travel-literature it is still fairly uncommon, outside the writings of Ibn Batuta and other well-known Arabs, to find accounts of travellers coming to the West from the East; this book, beautifully-produced with color illustrations, is a welcome addition to the list.

East Sails West deals with an almost-unknown voyage made by a Chinese junk to London, beginning at the end of 1846 and ending, rather sadly, with the breaking-up of the ship nine years later in the Liverpool docks.

The *Keying* had a mixed English-Chinese crew (an English captain, Charles Kellett, and a Chinese sailing-master, So Yin Sang Hsi); its voyage was financed by a group of Hong Kong merchants who hoped to stage an exhibition of its cargo of Chinese artefacts in London, cashing in, they hoped, on a burgeoning interest in things oriental. They even brought along a troupe of jugglers to entertain visitors on deck.

On the way, however, the *Keying* ran into trouble with the weather and with the ship itself, and was forced to divert the voyage to New York and Boston, which led to further problems and disputes over the payment of wages to the Chinese crew.

After some initial success in London with the exhibition (Queen Victoria visited the ship), the *Keying* was put up for auction in 1853; two years later it disappeared, along with most of the Chinese crew, whose fates are unknown.

The book is divided by Stephen Davies into three parts, which deal with the actual voyage and crew, the technical side of the story, and the aftermath of the voyage. The second part may be fully accessible only to specialists and maritime buffs, but it is thoroughly-researched and is exactly what a reader might expect from Stephen Davies, who was Director of the Hong Kong Maritime Museum and is now an honorary Fellow of the Hong Kong Institute for the Humanities and Social Sciences at the University of Hong Kong.

Mr. Davies provides a wealth of technical information, including tables of leg distance and speed, duration of the various legs of the voyage, and dimensions of the ship, as well as line diagrams and the color plates. He has, as a reviewer pointed out, an encyclopedic knowledge of ships and sailing, and there are few details left out in Mr. Davies's discussion of the shape, dimensions and speed of the *Keying*. Readers are presented with a great deal of information on such matters as how far junks could sail, what the daily life on the voyage was like; there is even a detailed comparison of the way Western and Chinese shipboard routine was managed and how well the crews performed during the voyage.

However, for most readers the main interest of the book will be the human and cultural aspects of the *Keying* adventure, and here also Mr. Davies does not disappoint.

The relationship between the Chinese and English crewmen is examined in detail, as well as the role of Charles Kellett, the captain of the ship. Mr. Davies has done meticulous research on the fate of the Chinese crewmen, particularly He Sing and So Yin Sang Hsi, one of what Mr. Davies calls "two final, sad elements to this story," the other being what happened to the cultural artifacts that the *Keying* was carrying. In fact, even Mr. Davies is not entirely sure what went on, as "one of the sorriest parts of the *Keying*'s story is how little we know of the stories of the Chinese crew." We don't even know why they signed up for the voyage or exactly what transpired when some of them found themselves in England with no ship. Mr. Davies even managed to find a sketch (from the log-book of HMS Actaeon) showing a Chinese "elder" being forced by a marine to kneel and kowtow to a Union Jack in front of British soldiers; the unfortunate man is identified as "Hising, who has been in England."

Some crewmen may have melted way into the Chinese community in London, and of course many remained in New York after the pay-dispute. Mr. Davies considered that Captain Kellet's decision to divert the voyage to the United States "was the decision of a fine and prudent seaman," which "very possibly saved [the crew] from death," but it didn't bring them much joy in their lawsuit for arrears of pay.

In spite of all good intentions on both sides, the reader is left with the impression that the Chinese got the worst end of the bargain.

It was true that the *Keying* accomplished what no Chinese ship had ever done before, namely sailed to the West, but the project failed in the end, as the ship and its crew disappeared into the mists of history and virtual oblivion, leaving few traces behind. Any kind of "cultural co-operation," as we would term it today, was purely accidental, as Mr. Davies rather wistfully has it, "the result was as ships passing in the night."

Before the *Keying*, the maritime world was Western; Britannia ruled the waves in terms of naval power, and when people thought of travel and exploration the names that came up would all have been Western, particularly Spanish, Portuguese, English, French or Venetian. The Ottomans, for example, had not been a significant naval power since their defeat at Lepanto in 1572. Non-western countries, it was reasoned, failed to meet the maritime grade because of sloth, incompetence or corruption.

In 1846 China was seen as a cultural backwater, and the voyage of the *Keying* was ignored. Indeed, as Mr. Davies notes, it still is. "No corporation has seen in the saga a vector for publicity," he tells us, "No TV or film company has been provoked to a froth of excitement by the prospect of a gripping docu-drama series and lucrative tie-ins."

The *Keying* episode was, in the end, fated to be part of what Mr. Davies calls

> the half-world of Western imperialism's many awkward, often not entirely successful (because mutually racist) working compromises—the world most Western and Chinese workaday people inhabited most of the time during that awkward epoch.

We owe a debt of gratitude to Mr. Davies for showing us this half-world and for bringing this adventure some of the publicity it surely deserves.

East Sails West: The Voyage of the Keying, 1846–1855, Stephen Davies (Hong Kong University Press, November 2013)

The Lone Flag: Memoir of the British Consul in Macau during World War II by John Pownall Reeves, edited by Colin Day and Richard Garrett

reviewed by Bill Purves

26 April 2014 — Portugal was neutral in World War II, and the Axis powers were anxious that it should remain so. As a result, even after Timor Leste's neutrality was ignored by the Allies, the Japanese continued to respect that of Macau. That made Britain's pre-existing Macau consulate the only one to remain in service in the Far East between the Soviet Union and Australia, except for those in China. John Reeves was the vice-consul there who kept that lone flag flying. The Royal Asiatic Society has together with Hong Kong University Press now published Reeves's memoir of his wartime experiences.

Regrettably, he began writing in 1945 immediately after the war's end and had completed the manuscript by 1949 when Macau's post-war status was still in doubt and Reeves was still in the Foreign Service. His revelations would in any case have required vetting by the Foreign Office, so Reeves's account is less than half of the story.

He focuses on his efforts to assist the 300,000 or so who took refuge in Macau after the fall of Hong Kong. They were British citizens, mostly Chinese, who had some family or other connection with Macau which the Japanese used as an excuse to push them out of Hong Kong to ease the shortage of food and fuel. Reeves describes his efforts to house and feed them and the parallel medical system he helped set up to meet their many needs. He claims that overall the refugee death rate was lower than that among refugees in London before the war.

Whitehall supported him financially throughout. There was no mail; the only contact with the outside world was through encoded radio messages. But the British government was able to transfer funds in the ordinary way through a bank in Lisbon.

How Reeves found anything to buy, however, is left unexplained. Presumably the remittances eventually supported a network of smugglers and other war profiteers. They also supported the Japanese war effort, as the Japanese were able to print army scrip and exchange it for hard currency in Macau, another reason, presumably, why its neutrality was respected.

Apart from his official duties, Reeves recounts some of the social life of the colony during the war. Even Portuguese wine was scarce, but sports, amateur performances and tea dances were apparently popular.

All this is interesting as far as it goes, but Reeves's presumably much more interesting anti-Japanese activities are alluded to only occasionally, and very, very indirectly. He mentions only that the Japanese offered a £4000 bounty for his assassination and that he was protected by plain-clothed Chinese nationalist troops as well as his own paid bodyguard. He claims to have been involved in smuggling about 300 Allied partisans through the Japanese lines to free China, but only his handling of one party of downed American airmen is described in any detail.

So don't purchase this memoir for tales of hugger-mugger, but *The Lone Flag* nevertheless gives an interesting picture of wartime life in a theatre which has previously received almost no attention.

The Lone Flag: Memoir of the British Consul in Macau during World War II, John Pownall Reeves, edited by Colin Day and Richard Garrett (Hong Kong University Press, April 2014)

An Anatomy of Chinese: Rhythm, Metaphor, Politics by Perry Link

reviewed by Loh Su Hsing

22 April 2014 — The latest book by Perry Link is an enjoyable exploration for anyone who is literate in Mandarin Chinese or has attempted to learn the language. It is a revealing read even for native speakers who might lack introspection and take many characteristics of the language for granted (including yours truly). Replete with examples from various contexts that are dished out with a subtle sense of humor, *An Anatomy of Chinese* is thoughtfully written and Link's passion for the language is both evident and infectious.

Analyzing phrases from the vernacular to officialese (the parts on double-entendre are particularly interesting), Link delves into inherent rhythms, spatial metaphors, philosophy of language, language cognition and how the ambiguity of Chinese language sometimes serves officials and citizens alike, who appropriate it for their own purposes. His analysis often points out salient observations such as how phrases are conferred authority (and sometimes even an "implicit claim to moral weight") simply because of their form even if the exact meaning and definition of these phrases remain vague—in addition to the examples listed in the book, 科学发展观 (Scientific Development Outlook, which is attributed to ex-President Hu Jintao) and 中国特色社会主义 (Socialism with Chinese Characteristics, the official ideology of the Chinese Communist Party) comes to mind.

Link highlights several aspects of the evolution of modern Chinese language, in particular, the "noun-borrowing" from English and argues that

> This influx of polysyllabic, Western-derived abstractions into the Chinese language played a major role in the formation of modern official Chinese...

> the distinctive flavor of modern official Chinese—simultaneously austere and vacuous, intimidating yet elusive, in short stuffy and puffy at the same time—owes its foundations to European habits of abstract conception that were brought into Chinese in the late nineteenth century.

While Link has put forth strong cases for all of his hypotheses, one cannot help but notice that 七言 and 五言 (translated as "seven speakings" and "five speakings" respectively by Link) are markedly less used by Chinese speakers outside of mainland China which somewhat undermines Link's argument that these are inherent preferred rhythms of the Chinese language. However, his observation that Mao had a particularly strong penchant for "seven speakings" and "five speakings" might explain its prevalence in modern China.

In his dissection of the Chinese language, Link has boldly unraveled an impressive range of topics while keeping his analysis accessible and engaging. The main merit of the book lies not just in the incisive propositions put forth, but also the questions that it raises and the line of inquiry that it opens lingers long after the book is closed.

Anatomy of Chinese: Rhythm, Metaphor, Politics, Perry Link (Harvard University Press, February 2013)

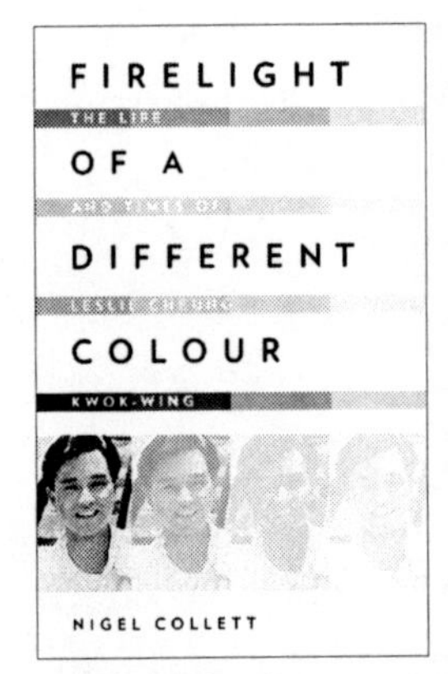

Firelight of a Different Colour: The Life and Times of Leslie Cheung Kwok-wing by Nigel Collett

reviewed by Peter Gordon

16 April 2014 — There was very little springlike about Hong Kong in March 2003: the city was in the grip of the SARS epidemic. We had, I remember, gotten the Literary Festival in just under the wire: the extent and seriousness of the disease was right then becoming evident. Schools were closed. The city was also facing a financial crisis. The mood was grim.

Although one knew, rationally, that there was no relation between these broader crises and the suicide of Hong Kong pop and movie star Leslie Cheung Kwok-wing on 1 April that year, it was hard at the time not to feel that it was ominous, even for those of us who were not among his legions of fans.

It was in fact a sort of turning point, although not the one feared at the time. Hong Kong's self-confidence bottomed out as SARS quickly receded and the city pulled out of the malaise that had been gripping it. But it, and events soon after, seemed to mark the final passing of a Hong Kong still linked to a colonial past.

Nigel Collett's new biography of Leslie Cheung, *Firelight of a Different Colour*, is in many ways as much the story of Hong Kong of the two or three decades leading up to that point as it is of the actor and singer himself.

It was a time of a great flowering of local culture—Cantopop and Hong Kong movies exploded into regional and sometimes international prominence; local stars became international mega-stars—as well as being the heyday of such icons as the Far Eastern Economic Review.

It was also, despite this vibrancy, a time of considerable existential angst as the 1997 Handover loomed. It can seem faintly absurd now, with the benefit of hindsight, that someone like Leslie Cheung would, as so many Hong Kong people did, pick up sticks and move to Canada; it didn't then. Cheung, again like many others, returned. He also, like much of Hong Kong, reconciled himself and his career aspirations to the new reality, although not always without some misgivings.

In Collett's biography, Cheung comes across to be a personification of much of this history:

> For nearly three decades, as the city had matured and risen to the world status it now possesses, as its language and culture had crystallized on cinema and TV screen, Leslie had been at the forefront of its art and its music, forging simultaneously his own artistic destiny while he wove the potent and magical blend of East and West which became Hong Kong's soul.

This is no rags-to-riches story—his family was reasonably well-off—but Cheung had a troubled childhood and difficult relationships with educational institutions as well as his parents. His success as an entertainer was hardly pre-ordained; Collett expounds at some length on Cheung's work ethic which was instrumental to this success.

Cheung's career overlapped the rise of the Hong Kong music and film industries, a rise in which he was very much a part, and their subsequent decline as they became something of casualty of their own success. This is the Hong Kong story in microcosm: careers and businesses built on the local market, expansion to China and elsewhere as globalization takes hold, following by the buffeting from international markets and competition, with only the truly international operations surviving. Cheung, although it is perhaps still a bit too early to be certain, seemed to be one of these.

Cheung's sexual orientation is of course also central to any discussion of the man and his work.

> He was openly gay and in this he was also unique... Alone in the world of Hong Kong stardom, he had prised open the closet door.

Collett covers the matter in detail. It can be hard to disentangle cause and effect, whether Leslie Cheung changed Hong Kong or whether he was fortunate to have been in the public eye just at the time when attitudes started to change, but one way or the other, Hong Kong is now a far more sophisticated place than it was three decades ago.

The family had no wish to cooperate with the author in the writing of this book; it is not, therefore, an "authorized" biography. And, its 700 footnotes notwithstanding, *Firelight of a Different Colour* is also not an academic work of, say, film history and analysis. But neither is it the sort of popular biography one might find on the way to the supermarket checkout: Collett makes sparing use of exclamation marks, for example, while tapping a vocabulary that includes such words as "obfuscate" and "vernacular"; there are also no photos, although one imagines the latter may be result of copyright issues.

The result—due in part to the quality of Collett's prose, which readers of *The Asian Review of Books* will already be familiar with—is a cogent, clear and, above all, respectful discussion of the man and his work, but one which does nevertheless lie in what some readers—who might have come to the book expecting something else—may find an uncomfortable middle ground: too comprehensive and meticulous in its coverage of the details of Cheung's career for those who wish a breezy read about an pop culture icon, while also not attempting to be a work of film criticism. Collett evidently intended neither—the book is not, he states a bit over-modestly in the introduction, a "full biography" but only "a first step". The depth of Collett's research will make the next researcher or writer's job considerably easier.

Further, the detail is integral to Collett's "attempt to understand Leslie's achievement and the cause of his death." What he seems to have demonstrated is that until the last few months of Cheung's life, there was apparently very little indication, even in retrospect, that he would have spiralled down so far and so fast. The attempt to understand, therefore, is perhaps ongoing.

But to see *Firelight of a Different Colour* as just a recounting of the life and career of Leslie Cheung is, I think, to miss the fact that in this exhaustive account Collett has retold—from a unique and illuminating perspective—the story of one of Hong Kong's most transformative periods. Hong

Kong has always been more than a place of business and politics. Chinese-speakers of course need no reminding of this; the rest of us perhaps do from time to time.

Nigel Collett reviews regularly for *The Asian Review of Books*.

Firelight of a Different Colour: The Life and Times of Leslie Cheung Kwok-Wing, Nigel Collett (Signal 8 Press, February 2014)

Forgotten Voices of Mao's Great Famine, 1958-1962: An Oral History by Zhou Xun

reviewed by Jonathan Chatwin

9 April 2014 — Following Yang Jisheng's *Tombstone* (2012) and Frank Dikötter's *Mao's Great Famine* (2010), it seemed that the horrors of the Great Leap Forward had, barring future archival revelations, been accounted in sufficient detail. Those two volumes exhaustively documented, over many hundreds of pages, the appalling consequences of the agricultural reform implemented by the Communists in the late 1950s.

While ostensibly intended to encourage China's productivity towards the levels of Russia and leading Western states, these reforms ultimately engendered the deaths, through starvation and violent enforcement of the party line, of between thirty and fifty million people. *Mao's Great Famine* and *Tombstone* seem definitive accounts, complementing each other to make the story of the Great Leap Forward as real as such an incomprehensible disaster can be made.

In some ways, Zhou's work could be seen as a companion piece to these bigger, narrative histories of the Great Leap Forward; where *Mao's Great Famine* and *Tombstone* deal with the famine on a national and provincial level, Zhou's comparatively slimmer work relates the stories of individuals who have survived the famine. Compelled by a desire to "record the past experiences and memories of those who are still alive before they too pass on," Zhou travelled around rural China collecting, over the course of four years, interviews with famine survivors. Aside from grouping these interviews into thematic chapters, with titles such as "Starvation and Death" and "Surviving the Famine", Zhou largely leaves the survivors to tell their own story; at an estimate, eighty-percent of the book is direct transcription. There are authorial intercessions, to clarify or provide historical backgrounds, but primacy is ceded to the first-hand accounts.

All of which seems laudable enough, but Zhou's approach—however worthy—renders the book unsatisfying to actually read.

There are a number of related reasons for this. First, the narrative of the Great Leap Forward, at an individual level, is not dramatic in a conventional sense; other historians, perhaps realizing this, have focused on the chronology of the catastrophe, on how the momentum built on the back of misguided policy decisions, either at provincial or national level. Zhou's decision to structure her work thematically sacrifices this sense of momentum, leaving the interviewees themselves with the job of sustaining the reader's interest, which they just about manage on a page-by-page level. Yet, there is no sense of one being compelled to read on—and the inevitable repetition of similar stories of hunger and poverty leads the reader to become somewhat desensitized to the inherent tragedy.

Narrative momentum is also not helped by the slightly clunky way in which Zhou endeavors to help the reader keep track of the different voices, and thus provide some continuity. When reintroducing interviewees from earlier chapters, she gives a short potted history of the individual, such as: "Qiaoer, the woman from Huang county in Shandong province, whose parents refused to comply with an order of the commune." This strategy, again a byproduct of the book's thematic structure, rarely works, tending to make the narrative even more stilted.

It may well be that Zhou never intended *Forgotten Voices* as anything more than a repository of the accounts she compiled over four years of clearly arduous research, and clearly the deficiencies identified are, to an extent, inherent in the form of oral history. Yet, though Zhou's tenacity and integrity should be applauded, the fact remains that, whatever the raw value of the testimonies collected in *Forgotten Voices*, the narrative of the Great Leap Forward has been told more powerfully and compellingly elsewhere.

Forgotten Voices of Mao's Great Famine, 1958-1962: An Oral History, Xun Zhou (Yale University Press, November 2013)

Gao Xingjian: Painter of the Soul by Daniel Bergez

reviewed by Loh Su Hsing

10 March 2014 — Faced with a lengthy monograph dedicated to Nobel Prize for Literature laureate Gao's painted *oeuvre*, some readers may question whether their attention is not being wasted on a gifted writer's hobbyistic sideline.

Perceptively, Bergez provides the required *captatio benevolentiae* by showing that Gao has from early childhood cultivated his dual vocation with equal dedication—he illustrated his very first piece of fiction himself—and that the evolution of his visual style from figurativeness to lyrical abstraction and finally "expressive minimalism" is informed by a rich internalized dialectic between not only East and West but also tradition and modernism.

Gao's position at these multiple "crossroads" is broken down into biographical, philosophical and more importantly technical elements, such as the use of ink on canvas instead of paper or quasi-abstract figurativeness, to establish the painter's "exceptional originality" and further justify admiring and studying his creations for their own merits, independently from any echoes one may find in them of the novelist's *Soul Mountain* and other masterpieces. Gao's own essays, in particular *Another Kind of Aesthetics*, are cited in support of this "anti-intellectual" approach to painting, which "begins where language fails" and exists entirely in sphere of "direct perception", to the extent that, for the artist, assigning a title to his canvases often proves a challenge.

Bergez insists on the necessity to "experience" Gao's paintings rather than to scrutinize them for possible meanings, and he is most successful in preserving the immediacy he advocates when identifying key recurring motives such as the circle and the vertical linear line or describing the viewer's sense of spatial instability. The numerous and careful reproductions, mostly from Gao's recent period, play a key part in approximating the experience of standing in front of "The House in a Dream" or "The Celestial Eye".

However, there is an element of frustration in reading Bergez's repeated assertions that "fragile words are incapable of describing an artist's visual world" when this is precisely what he is attempting in his essay, and with his self-imposed refusal to give his writing any kind of interpretative dimension. In equally disconcerting fashion, while insisting on placing Gao's visual creations in an autonomous sphere, Bergez relies heavily on the novelist to explain the painter, as in this passage from *Soul Mountain*: "While pretending to understanding, I still don't understand."

With less paralyzing reverence, Bergez—to quote the title of his previous book, *Painting and Writing: A Dialogue of the Arts*—could have established a more open and fruitful "dialogue" between Gao's literary and visual accomplishments, rendering the monograph a more satisfying experience.

Gao Xingjian: Painter of the Soul, Daniel Bergez, Sherry Buchanan (trans.) (Asia Ink/Asia Society, March 2014)

Following the Leader: Ruling China, from Deng Xiaoping to Xi Jinping by David M Lampton

reviewed by Kerry Brown

2 March 2014 — I remember once reading through the transcript of a meeting between the then President Jiang Zemin and a visiting British delegation. His style of speech was, to put it gently, elliptical. He roved from literary to personal references, wandering on and off subject, speaking with evident passion but about issues which most people did not expect to hear in such rarefied company.

David Lampton in his account of Jiang's visit to the US in the 1980s when mayor of Shanghai captures something of this. When asked what he most wanted to learn about Chicago, Jiang replied "Sewerage". He wanted to know how a city of similar size and complexity as his own dealt with waste water efficiently.

One of the striking, but almost certainly unintended, effects reading *Following the Leader*, an account of top level leadership in China over the last three decades is to be struck by the vapidness of a lot of elite interaction and discussion, at least going from some of the accounts set down here.

Jiang is one relatively bright spot in a fairly bland menu of conversational platitudes and stereotypical poses. It seems that when America's top leaders and delegations meet with Chinese they clam up and come out with rehearsed positions and the safest of safe statements.

Lampton states in his introduction that one of the unique features of his account is that it is based on a large archive of recordings of leadership statements and discussions, the vast majority between US and Chinese interlocutors. Some of these were attended by Lampton himself in his long academic career, particularly during his time as President of the National

Committee of US China Relations.

But the sneaking worry that one is in fact witnessing two sides doing all they can to put the other off the scent never quite dissipates. As the book progresses through its themes of military, political and economic issues and how US observers saw Chinese leaders acting over these, there is a palpable sense that we have two partners who on the whole profoundly disagree with each other's world outlook, but have no choice but to work together. Only rarely, for instance, over issues like military expenditure do the conversations between US and China parties seem to get really heated. The rest of the time, it's mostly cordial agreeing to disagree.

The quantity of US-Chinese political engagement over the period that the book covers is not in question. Deng, Jiang, Hu and then Xi were all visited by copious US delegations, and each of them in turn had at least one, and in some cases several, visits to the US

In terms of quality, however, we have to be more circumspect. One useful service of Lampton's putting this all together is to give a relatively short audit of just how good the dialogue between the US and China at the elite political level has been over the last three decades. On many of the accounts here, it seems not to have been particularly searching or profound at all.

Perhaps this is as much to do with the values mindset. Lampton has an interesting discussion of this in terms of moral outlook and "situational ethics". He argues that this stops China from wanting to involve itself in anything that might not have direct bearing on its own national interests. But mindsets about China itself and what its essential nature is are also hard to put aside.

Lampton spends several pages decrying the lack of unity in the Chinese bureaucracy, and the disconnect he often sees between the party and government universes. This is a point made often in other places.

Even so, in view of the vast governance challenges of a country as huge and populous as China, perhaps the surprising thing is that it is as well governed as it is, and that in many ways the impact of elite decision making is far less extreme than we often think. On the whole, there is an argument to say that China is more suited to organic governance, rather than vertical fiat from a solid centre.

And a defender of China would say that the governance of the US is also often dysfunctional and chaotic—look at the government shut down in 2013. Isn't a commentator like Lamton showing precisely the sort of US superiority many Chinese commentators complain about?

Lampton refers to his ambition in this book of letting us see how the Chinese leaders themselves view the world.

I don't think this is what the book really tells us however. There is no doubt that it is packed with excellent evidence of how the US and Chinese leaders interacted. And it says a lot about how the US saw China over this period, and how its leaders talked to Americans.

But on how Chinese leaders really saw themselves, I don't think we learn very much.

That would have been a much more intimate book, and one which would have contained more material of how the Chinese leadership from the 1980s spoke amongst themselves. And the last people they would have wanted in the room when they were doing this were the leading political representatives of a country they often saw as their greatest competitor and the source of so many of their problems.

Following the Leader: Ruling China, from Deng Xiaoping to Xi Jinping, David M. Lampton (University of California Press, February 2014)

The Siege of Tsingtao by Jonathan Fenby

reviewed by Peter Gordon

20 February 2014 — This year marks the centenary of the outbreak of the First World War; rhetorical flourishes have already begun comparing the current Asian geopolitical situation to Europe in months before the assassination in Sarajevo. Japanese Prime Minister Shinzo Abe might not have been so quick to invoke 1914 in regard to China's relations with its neighbors had he first read Jonathan Fenby's new book *The Siege of Tsingtao*.

And at less than 70 pages—I read it on a single to-and-from commute to the office—there is really no excuse not to.

Tsingtao was the first and only battle of the World War One to be fought in East Asia. It is usually at most a footnote in histories of a conflict which resulted in unprecedented slaughter, spelled the end of Empire (the Austro-Hungarians, Ottomans and Romanovs all succumbing) and ushered in Bolshevism and Communism (immediately) and Fascism (not long after). But, Fenby argues, seen from an Asian perspective,

> The clash in Tsingtao forms part of a saga with a present-day resonance.

Tsingtao, being held by Germany, was an obvious military target. Japan accepted British overtures for a joint operation; the Japanese saw an opportunity for expansion.

> For [Foreign Minister] Kato and his colleagues this was not so much an attack on Germany under the alliance with Britain as a means of enlarging their country's position in China.

From that point on, the British hardly had a look in; British troops were made subordinate to Japanese command. After the German capitulation, the British Embassy in Tokyo was informed that "it would 'be more convenient for practical matters'" if matters were left to the Japanese troops. Japan appointed a Governor and that was that.

The Allied, that is Japanese, victory—never in doubt given Tsingtao's isolation—gave Japan leverage at the Versailles Peace Conference. At Versaille, as throughout the war, "Realpolitik reigned, at the expense of China."

Fenby connects the dots: much of what happened in the following three decades up to the Communist victory in 1949 can be attributed to ways the Japanese and Chinese were respectively treated at Versailles. Of course, China was not the only erstwhile ally on the wrong side of secret treaties (the Arabs have similar long-term grudges against the Sykes-Picot agreement) and the Japanese trajectory to attempted regional hegemony predated Tsingtao by at least a couple of decades.

The Siege of Tsingtao's brevity is admirable. Fenby quotes liberally and pithily from primary sources—upon hearing of the Japanese ultimatum to quit the city, for example, an anonymous German huffed in his diary that "They can tell this to a Russian but not to a German". He gives rousing and evocative descriptions of the battles themselves and an inside look at the various diplomatic machinations and misgivings. Cables from the Kaiser, monogrammed cigarettes from the Japanese Emperor, batlike German airplanes and the first recorded air-sea battle and are the sort of piquant and picturesque details in which this slim volume abounds. The Japanese's lack of respect for their erstwhile British allies was palpable and even explicit, something that should and did ring warning bells for the future.

Fenby also sets the event firmly in its historical context, fore and aft. The book is a useful refresher for period from the last decades on the nineteenth century through the mid-point of the twentieth. Japan, Germany and Russia all get their due.

Fenby's account of the Japanese attack on Tsingtao—and it was mostly Japanese, the British playing a minor supporting role—reads eerily like the Japanese invasion of Hong Kong in the next war: naval landings, bombing and bombardment of the urban areas, the progressive abandoning of defensive lines, the messages from the government back home encouraging the brave yet futile defense in the face of hopelessness of it all, the ultimate surrender. Tsingtao seems—albeit anachronistically—like a practice run.

Any complaints? Well, one. The editing style seems to exclude commas in large numbers, so—except for a lone comma in "4,700" on page 6—one is left counting zeroes in "55000" and "550000" to figure out how many that actually was.

That very minor point aside, not only is *The Siege of Tsingtao* the sort of consumable publication that might make books once again common on public transport, it should also serve secondary schools and universities, especially in Greater China, as an engaging essay illustrating how seemingly isolated events often aren't.

The Siege of Tsingtao, Jonathan Fenby (Penguin China, February 2014)

Taming Tibet: Landscape Transformation and the Gift of Chinese Development by Emily T. Yeh

reviewed by Kerry Brown

27 January 2014 — Tibet remains the most intimidatingly politicized of all issues for those trying to understand contemporary China and its internal dynamics and realities, so *Taming Tibet*, Emily Yeh's study, based on extensive long term field research and engagement, is timely and important.

Readers should persist through the somewhat abstract tone with which the book starts, clogged up with various theoretical phrases and explanations, to get to the excellent chapters which follow: on the vegetable market economy dominated by migrants in the region; the ways in which many ethnic urban Tibetans almost seem to deliberately disenfranchise themselves from the "market rationalism" system and end up under-employed or unemployed; and the support by the central state of development gifts through housing projects and highly visible schemes which serve, on one hand, to manufacture indebtedness by locals but also serve as one of the few means by which they can score back at a central state they resent and feel coerced by accepting freebies from it.

The issue of Tibet, because of the challenge of access to it, is one that has not had the sophisticated, nuanced treatment it deserves. This book goes some way to rectifying that, and should enjoy wide circulation. It sets out the complexity unvarnished: crude pro- or anti-authority postures are resisted.

Among the dominant narratives it resists is that somehow pre-1949, Tibet was an undeveloped backwater led by political dinosaurs and that afterwards it was liberated into an enlightened era of developmentalism and modernity. Yeh makes clear that the modernity supported over the last half century in the region has neither been straightforward nor uniform, nor, for that matter, was it the only option. It was the result of choices, made by people who were pursuing specific aims, and most of the time who were very remote from the region. Their vision of modernity, however well meaning, did not preclude other options and paths the region could have taken. Yeh certainly doesn't waste time defending how Tibet had been pre-PRC control, and nor does she wade into the endless arguments over historic legitimacy. Her preoccupation is with how people from different backgrounds in the region now are actually engaging with modernity, and her conclusions are sobering ones.

Tibet is an important place to understand because, as Yeh eloquently puts it, "it provides a distinctive and revealing view of the [central] state." The consensus of this state over the last three decades is largely that market rationality is the primary tool of development, and that a model which has been very successful in creating wealth in other parts of the country can be used in a place whose geography, culture and society are as distinctive as in Tibet. This is a contentious assumption, and one that Yeh looks at in some detail purely in terms of how state subsidies operate in the region. Scholars like Ma Rong have argued that Tibet is highly reliant on central government money and that it exists in many ways as a dependent region of the country. Yeh looks at the ways in which migrant laborers, many from Sichuan, come to the area, work primarily in centrally subsidized construction and vegetable farming, and usually send much of the wealth they generate back out of the local economy. If the objective therefore is to create sustainable wealth in the region, therefore, structurally there seems to be a major flaw at the moment.

But there are more profound challenges, and these relate to the ways in which Tibetans she interviews paint themselves as lazy, "spoilt" and unable to work in ways that Han temporary migrants do. On the surface, this looks like a group of people beating up on themselves. But Yeh describes interpret this as a deliberate act of disenfranchisement, something highly political in which Tibetans are almost opting out of the state-mandated template of agency that has been offered to them. This resistance is highly subtle, and something that Yeh links to other subaltern communities elsewhere in the world, but it is one that operates in a context of increased political sensitivity and danger since the riots of 2008 as one of the lowest risk forms of passive protest. It is also, tragically, one that has created deeper dependency and more poverty for many local people.

Yeh's final chapters are on the ways in which "gifts" of development and modernity via the route of improved housing in the region, and the vast process of urbanization (urban/rural and the divide between them are, in fact, concepts that Yeh fascinatingly shows simply did not exist in Tibet prior to the creation—through government policy and aid support—of large numbers of towns in the 1990s) have created restrictive structures for local agency. People are simply given inducements, not physically violent but restrictive and silently coercive, to adopt particular lifestyles and modes of behavior. The need to have visible success for the central state's development agenda in the region is seen in the "comfortable housing" projects that many people have been moved into in the last decade. These have all figured as part of the national plan since 2005 to create a "socialist modern countryside".

This is a rich, stimulating and rewarding study, and raises broader questions about how modernity can sit beside preserving the investment people make in tradition in order to derive their identity, something that has relevance far beyond China's borders.

It is also a study that pushes the reader to move beyond narratives of victimhood and oppressor that often occur in treatments of Tibet. It shows that the central state in fact has some difficult choices to make about its policy, and that an emphasis purely on economics is going to be unsustainable. The profound issues that Tibet raises about the values and culture of the central state and its eventual vision of society are important across China.

It is unlikely that this book will be read sympathetically in Beijing, but that is a pity. It is a balanced, empirically-grounded and hugely suggestive study, and one that I could not commend more highly.

Taming Tibet: Landscape Transformation and the Gift of Chinese Development, Emily T. Yeh (Cornell University Press, November 2013)

Italy's Encounters with Modern China by Maurizio Marinelli and Giovanni Andornino (eds.)

reviewed by Angelo Paratico

24 January 2014 — *Italy's Encounters with Modern China* is a collection of short essays dealing, true to its title, with various aspects of political, military and social interactions between Italy and China. The starting point is the founding of Italy in 1861; by the final chapters, the papers cover what is basically contemporary history.

A work like this is long overdue. Nothing of such depth has been published before and the high level of research put together by the ten academics contributing to this project is remarkable.

One hopes that the collection will be translated into Italian and made available for Italians wishing to know more about these aspects of their history, which have been so far been kept rather hidden. Only since Italian president Giorgio Napolitano visited the former Italian concession of Tianjin in 2010, has it been acceptable to speak about Italy's Eastern colonial exploits. Only then did the vast majority of Italians discover—from newspaper reports and television programs—that a square kilometer of what is today the sprawling metropolis of Tianjin had been a part of Italy, with a Via Vittorio Emanuele III and a Piazza Regina Elena, and a public fountain in the middle, the first ever built in China. Fascism (1922-1943) figured heavily in Italy's nationalistic expansion, leaving a sort of blemish attached to it; after Fascism's fall, it became safer to dismiss the whole matter, without trying to separate what was history from what was simple machismo.

The book's first chapters, describing what was then called "the scramble for concessions" are particularly fresh and interesting. British and French sources imply that the part by played by Italy in such military aggression had been negligible. This is not completely true; a possible explanation for the lack of information lies in the fact that next to nothing had been translated from Italian. Sources are indeed available in Italian, but are dispersed in hundreds of booklets, personal memoirs or marginal travelogues, which are difficult to locate in libraries and were not reprinted after WWII.

I found singularly well-researched and interesting the chapters dealing with Italy's military intervention in 1900, alongside the armies of the United States, Russia, Japan, France, Great Britain, Austria, and Germany, to free the diplomatic legations put under siege by the Boxers: an incredible feat for a nation like Italy, still very poor and with millions of its citizens forced abroad to work in what amounts to a diaspora. Colonialism, back then, to some seemed an answer to such huge problems.

A number of historians have laid the blame for the Boxer uprising squarely on Italy's shoulders, accusing the country of excessive ambition—as Jung Chang appears to do in her somewhat fictionalized biography of Empress Cixi—but this is an exaggeration. Italy was still reeling from the 1896 defeat at Adowa by the Ethiopians, when it asked China for large territorial concessions. In a grave miscalculation, Italy was counting on British support, which did not materialize. This grotesque story was related by the Times's correspondent George Morrison in his correspondence from Beijing. China flatly refused Italy's demands and the Italian minister for Foreign Affairs, Napoleone Canevaro, cabled for an ultimatum to be presented to China. The British Ambassador in Rome, alarmed, demanded it to be withdrawn. Canevaro then sent a second cable asking that the ultimatum not be presented. But the second message being shorter than the first, it reached Beijing earlier than the first one containing the full text of the ultimatum. The Italian representative in Beijing, Renato De Martino, first received a cable instructing him not to present the ultimatum, then a second with an ultimatum and instructions to present it. Close to a nervous breakdown, he presented it.

China again ignored the provocation as if nothing had happened and after the 48 hours set by the ultimatum expired, Italy realized it could do nothing but lose face. De Martino was dismissed and Napoleone Canevaro resigned. The other powers took the position that China concluded that it could ignore their demands as it did Italy's, so Italy was therefore to blame for what was to follow.

Newcomers to the subject, however, might wish to be reminded of some of the interesting elements of Italy and Italians in China. The influence of Italy in China grew after WWI and reached its apogee with the arrival of Edda Mussolini, the Duce's first-born, together with her husband, Galeazzo Ciano (1903-1944) appointed consul of Italy in Shanghai. They became one of the most prominent and talked about couples in China, with tales of binges, gambling and sexual escapades. The British secret service fabricated a story of a sexual liaison between Ciano and Wallis Simpson, also living there, in the vain hope of discouraging the Prince of Wales from marrying her.

Galeazzo Ciano's first diplomatic posting was in Beijing, before his engagement to Mussolini; he came to Shanghai in 1930 and remained until 1933. All the gossip notwithstanding, he did a good job; the fruits of his labor—extremely difficult in a period of constant Japanese provocation—were many. One was the creation of a joint-venture SINAW (Sino-Italian National Aircraft Works) at Nanchang, Jiangxi Province, from 1933 through 1936. Training in Italy was offered to several pilots and technicians in order to allow them read charts and instruments written in Italian. It ended badly, bombed by Japanese planes, in spite of the Italian flag on the roof. Another of Ciano's achievements was the establishment of a shipping line connecting Trieste and Shanghai. The first sailing was in 1932 with the deluxe liners Conte Verde and Conte Rosso, which set a record time of 23 days trip.

Ciano was once approached outside the Cathay Hotel by an old woman who wanted to read his hand. He asked her with nonchalance: "When will I die?" She replied: "At forty, by a violent death." There are letters by Ciano in which he brags about that forecast, which proved to be correct

The only thing wanting in *Italy's Encounters with Modern China* is a bibliography which should have been treated as a separate chapter. This would have made this book an indispensable tool for Italian and foreign historians interested in this chapter of the expansion of Europe into the Far East.

Italy's Encounters with Modern China; Imperial Dreams, Strategic Ambitions, Giovanni Andornino, Maurizio Marinelli (eds.) (Palgrave Macmillan, November 2013)

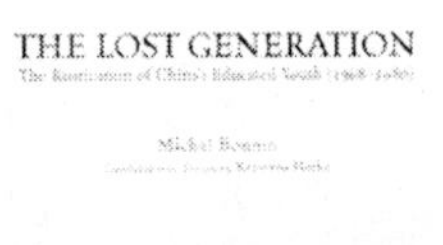

Lost Generation: The Rustification of Chinese Youth (1968-1980) by Michel Bonnin

reviewed by Kerry Brown

16 January 2014 — The current elite leadership of contemporary China is from the "sent down" generation. Xi Jinping, whose father was felled in the early 1960s, spent most of his youth in rural Shaanxi. Wang Qishan, his fellow Politburo member, stayed only a few kilometers from him, in the late part of the decade after the Cultural Revolution started in 1966, although it is unclear whether they ever knew each other from this time. Li Keqiang was rusticated, as the term goes, in his native Anhui.

Unlike their predecessors, who were in young adulthood when the Cultural Revolution started, Xi and his peers were in their teens and were the age group hit most forcibly by the Maoist plan of sending a whole generation from cities to various parts of the vast countryside. As Michel Bonnin makes clear in his comprehensive and richly-documented account of this generation, the outcomes from this unique decade long period of modern Chinese history were mixed, often traumatic, and left a profound impression on those who underwent the uprooting from their homes to some of the most backward, hostile environments in rural China.

Bonnin makes clear that the motivations behind the rustication campaign when it first started in the early 1960s were partly economic, but—perhaps more importantly—ideological. For Mao, the bureaucracy of the Party had grown fat and self-serving. A new elite had arisen on the ashes of the old. They were urban, looked after their children in elite educational facilities, and were straying a long way from the agrarian revolutionary roots of the Party and its rise to power. Intellectuals in particular, as they were configured in Mao's world view (he had briefly been a lowly librarian at Peking University and had seen the more haughty, unforgiving side of academic life in early 20th century China) were a problem that needed to be dealt with in increasingly radical ways from the early cleansing campaigns of the 1950s. Sending a whole generation of city youths to the countryside was one way of radicalizing and energizing the revolutionary instincts of the China young and winning them back to Mao's cause. In the end, it was his patronage that made this vast campaign possible.

Bonnin sets out the historic roots of the campaign, its antecedents in movements promoted in the Soviet Union under Khrushchev and their adaptation to China. Based on over four decades of research, this masterful volume, originally published in French in the early 2000s, and now excellently translated into English, sets out precise data for exactly how many were affected, but also shows where people went, what they did, and, perhaps most importantly of all, what they experienced.

The individual voices that Bonnin refers to make clear that for the vast majority, far from bridging the gap between the urban and rural spaces of China, the rustication campaign impeded economic development, created vast resentment (farmers were loath to spare their time to teach naïve city dwellers flooding their villages how to work when they had enough of a challenge supporting themselves) and was, both in terms of policy and its implantation, a failure.

Its failure was most dramatically shown by the vast numbers who voted with their feet in the late 1970s—when the Cultural Revolution ended and Mao had died—by revolting against their removal from the cities. Many from Shanghai who had ended up in Xinjiang rebelled, and there were links between this series of protests and the short lived Democracy Wall events in late 1978 into 1979 in Beijing. Unlike Democracy Wall and its hard core of activists who were ruthlessly crushed, the sent down youths were largely listened to, and many were allowed to return to where they had come from. The original Maoist vision, hopelessly Utopian and impractical, of youths being forever in a place they were forcibly sent to collapsed, as did so many other aspects of Maoism.

The longer term impact of this period however was in the attitudes of those who had been through this experience and survived. For them, distrust of the government and Party remained deep, and a feeling of cynicism set in. The Party based its legitimacy not on Romantic appeals to build a new world from the 1980s, but on making people wealthier. So far, this message has worked.

Bonnin's book reads like the life work it is, a scrupulously careful account of a unique and epic movement, but one that allows time and space to the voices of those who went through this experience. It is interesting to reflect on how this had an impact on the people now running China, especially in view of their fervent support for deeper and faster urbanization. For them, it seems, at least from the policy they are supporting, memories of the countryside are not warm, and the China they wish to build is a world away from the primitive, often hostile and harsh environment that many of their contemporaries had to live in for many years over four decades ago.

Lost Generation: The Rustification of Chinese Youth (1968-1980), Michel Bonnin (Chinese University Press, October 2012)

At Least We Lived by Emma Oxford; *In Time of War* by Lt. Cmdr. Henry CS Collingwood-Selby

reviewed by Peter Gordon

9 January 2014 — Lt. Cmdr. Henry Collingwood-Selby was recuperating in hospital on Christmas Day 1941; he noted in his diary entry for the day: "5:45 Heard news of surrender."

Collingwood-Selby's diary entries for the fateful year of 1941 are included in the recent *In Time of War*, a collection of his papers from the period, transcribed and edited by his son Richard. The publication of this volume coincides with Emma *Oxford's At Least We Lived: The Unlikely Adventures of an English Couple in World War II China*, the story of her parents and similarly based on personal papers. Her father, Max Oxford, was one of the small party who escaped from Hong Kong on that fateful Christmas day along with Chinese Admiral Chan Chak.

Max Oxford ended up in Chungking (now Chongqing), where he met Audrey Watson—the author's future mother—who had just been sent out from England to work in the Embassy. The dramatic highlight of *At Least We Lived* is the chapter on the Christmas Day escape. Admiral's Chan's escape had been planned ahead of time. He was spirited out of the Gloucester Hotel; there were Motor Torpedo Boats waiting on Ap Lei Chau, just off Aberdeen in the south of the Colony. They almost didn't make it: their launch was shot out from under them and they had to swim to Ap Lei Chau. They survived, met up with the boats, crossed Mirs Bay and went overland through enemy lines to Waichow (now Huizhou).

However, it is Audrey and Audrey's voice that dominates the rest of the book, perhaps because most of the source materials were her letters and journals. Emma Oxford is a sympathetic editor and narrator and is fortunate that her mother seems to have been both observant as well as loquacious. There is a certain Downton Abbey quality to the language: a place is described as "terribly dark and poky" and when recounting a meal in a Chinese "restaurant" [which Audrey places in quotes]:

> … it is every man for himself, and let the worst man starve. Then it is every man for himself. If you at all adept with chopsticks, you come away more than replete. Need I add that I became as adept as I could in the shortest possible time?

Modern personal communication usually pales by comparison. Audrey's observations can have a sharp or ironic edge to them:

> Why is it the French can talk so much better than the English? We had a cocktail before dinner and everyone was very gay, whilst the English drink gallons, become very stupid and dull, and eventually pass out.

One can't help thinking the material might serve as the basis of a novel or TV mini-series—one can almost hear Emma Thompson uttering these lines, making the result somewhat reminiscent of Olivia Manning's *Balkan Trilogy*.

Notwithstanding Max's heroics and adventures in Africa and the Middle East prior to coming to the Far East—he hobnobbed with the likes of Freya Stark in 1930s Baghdad, for example—the narrative is about such matters as how much things cost, cobbling together a marriage in wartime Chungking, the trials and tribulations of socializing and entertaining in Hong Kong after the War. Interesting—not least for the company they kept—but nevertheless rather quotidien. Indeed, the title comes from a journal entry, made after departing Hong Kong for good in 1951, referring not to the interesting times through which the couple lived but rather to the sort of life they led:

> At least I feel we have lived … I shall be glad to remember we have drunk champagne freely…

* * *

Collingwood-Selby had a rather different War: he was incarcerated first in the Argyle Street POW camp and then, from 1944, in Shamshuipo. The story told by *In Time of War* isn't always what one might have expected: Collingwood-Selby was evidently allowed considerable freedom of movement at least through mid-February 1942 and the experience of Argyle Street camp POWs appears not to have been as unremittingly horrendous as at others. It is also true that Collingwood-Selby seems to have made a consistent effort at looking on the brighter side of things when possible, commenting on nice weather, colorful birds and the views.

While the immediacy of these accounts is both interesting and appealing—good source material, again, for a novel should someone care to write one—the collection itself is largely unstructured: a narrative can be discerned, but that is evidently not the point of the publication. One has to question whether the materials might have been more profitably (for the reader, if not the publisher) placed online rather than in a physical book: this would have allowed searching and hyperlinked footnotes of which the book has 908(!), requiring incessant flipping back and forth.

Both books owe much to a previous generation's predilection not just for journal-keeping and letter-writing but also setting them aside for posterity. Wartime China, the powers of observation displayed by the subjects, and the serendipitous discovery of bundles of papers are not the only things that tie these books together: in an odd coincidence, Chile plays a central role in each: Audrey was born there, and Richard Collingwood-Selby, the son and editor, now lives there.

Hong Kong being such a small place, Max Oxford and Henry Collingwood-Selby might well have run into each other before one ended up in the camps and the other escaped, helping escort a Chinese admiral to Chungking. Our current Christmases are less eventful, thank goodness.

At Least We Lived: The Unlikely Adventures of an English Couple in World War II China, Emma Oxford (Branksome Books, August 2013); *In Time of War: Lt. Cmdr. Henry C.S. Collingwood-Selby, R.N. (1898-1992) and Others*, Lt. Cmdr. Henry C.S. Collingwood-Selby, R.N., Richard Collingwood-Selby and Gillian Bickley (eds) (Proverse, April 2013)

Voices from Tibet: Selected Essays and Reportage by Tsering Woeser and Wang Lixiong

reviewed by Kerry Brown

7 January 2014 — Since 2011, over 100 Tibetans have self-immolated. This act of political despair has highlighted the sense felt by many Tibetans living in the autonomous region and elsewhere in China that their cultural identity is under profound threat. The root of this is a vision of modernity adopted by the central government in Beijing which regards many of the religious practices and beliefs of a large number of ethnic Tibetans as backward and retrogressive. The narrative of Tibetan history before 1949 is presented in orthodox People's Republic historiography as one of feudal exploitation at the hands of lamas, with the annexation of 1959 as a moment of liberation.

Writing about Tibet is challenging because of the entrenched positions of many of the key stakeholders, the highly politicized nature of the region's status and international perceptions of it, and the battle between Beijing and various sections of the global community and individuals sympathetic to the plight of specific groups in Tibet over how to view the region.

The presentation of Tibet as an issue best seen in stark black and white moral terms derived from these two main contesting perspectives has long since been one of the main impediments to understanding what is really happening there and how best to interpret it. One antidote is to try to listen as hard as possible to the voices of those most directly affected by this long standing problem: the people of Tibet themselves.

Tsering Woeser must rank as one of the most globally respected and best known of such voices. She has spoken with great bravery and lucidity about issues concerning Tibet, and despite being based in Beijing, has managed to visit the region many times. She has also, remarkably, avoided some of the more heavy-handed interventions of the state security apparatus which has been so efficiently harsh on others who have attempted to speak out. Nor does she mince her words.

This slender volume (it has fewer than 100 pages) has articles on Tibet's history of colonization, the changing nature of Lhasa as it has been transformed from a religious centre to one largely geared up to accommodating large numbers of visiting tourists, and its relations with Beijing. She and her co-author, husband Wang Lixiong, also deal with the highly contentious issue of the choice of the Panchen Lama in 1995 when Beijing and the Dalai Lama chose different candidates. The detention by Beijing of the Dalai Lama's choice, a boy barely six at the time, meant that the unenviable record for the country with the world's youngest political prisoner went for many years to China.

This collection is furnished with a lengthy introduction by the ever excellent Robbie Barnett, a US-based academic who has been one of the most even-handed commentators and scholars of Tibet for many years, and who sets Wang and Woeser's essays in context. Both come from unique backgrounds: Wang is a long-term intellectual and activist who has had many tough scrapes with the authorities over the last three decades, and who remains one of the few non-Tibetan voices in China willing to engage with issues raised by the contentious status of the region in ways which stray from the usual rigid rhetoric used by many who speak it. Woeser was born in Lhasa during the Cultural Revolution, to parents who were of mixed Han and Tibetan ethnicity (her paternal grandfather was Han Chinese). That her father worked in the People's Liberation Army gives her work an extra angle—it is from someone who would well have joined to cozy elites from the Tibetan region who have accommodated to the status quo there, and never chosen to speak about the great challenges the region faces. Brought up in Sichuan, she moved to Beijing to study and has been based there ever since.

The essays in this collection, ably translated by Violet Law, are mostly from Internet articles. They are polemical in style, and highly accessible.

One issue they do raise sharply is the dearth of fresh ideas and new thinking about Tibet and its unique cultural, environmental and geopolitical issues, by political leaders in Beijing. It is clear that the current system of governance with its heavy reliance on security and diktat is unsustainable. But nor is there any viable solution from Tibetans themselves waiting in the wings. The Dalai Lama has proposed a middle-way policy, where autonomy is increased but sovereignty rejected.

But the issues of how to politically mediate power between a vast region which is currently a net burden on Chinese central fiscal funds, and an area where there are many specificities in terms of environment, governance and culture which a centralized administrative template can't address is far less easy to solve than many of Beijing's critics would like to admit.

This book helps a little in uncovering the nuances and complexities of Tibet in the 21st century, by three of the people—Barnett, Wang and Woeser—best-qualified to do this.

Voices from Tibet: Selected Essays and Reportage, Lixiong Wang Tsering Woeser (Hong Kong University Press, November 2013)

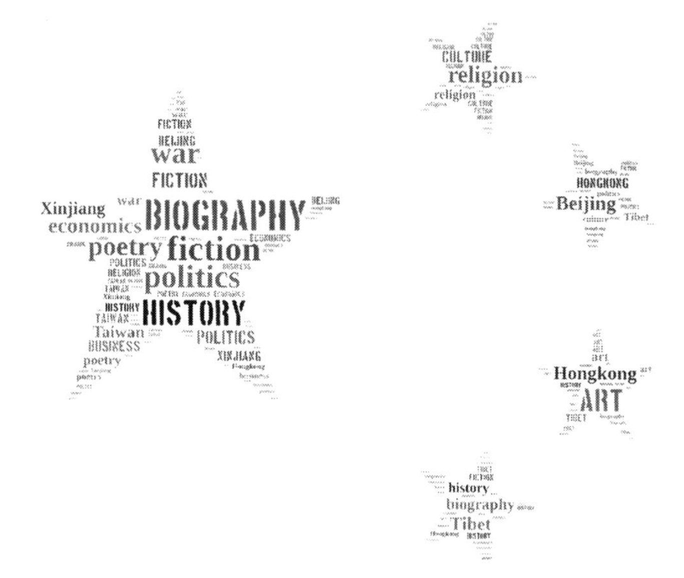
CULTURE
religion
religion
FICTION
BEIJING
war
FICTION
Xinjiang
BIOGRAPHY
economics
poetry
fiction
politics
HISTORY
Taiwan
BUSINESS
POLITICS
XINJIANG
HONGKONG
Beijing
Tibet
Hongkong
ART
history
biography
Tibet

Fiction

Black Holes by He Jiahong

reviewed by Peter Gordon

19 November 2014 — Crime fiction, whodunits and mysteries constitute one of the more diverse genres in English-language publishing. Not only are there all the books set in the author's home country, English-language writers have set entire series overseas (Martin Cruz Smith's *Gorky Park* comes to mind) or with atypical detectives in unusual locations or the past (the Cadfael series features a medieval monk as detective) while immigrant writers have set series in their home countries (for example, Qiu Xiaolong's Inspector Chen series).

Works in translation are less common and fundamentally different. Written a language other than English for a non-English-speaking audience, they provide a direct window into another culture, albeit one tinted by translation. There is Georges Simenon in French, of course, as well as the venerable Kobo Abe from Japan and his multiple successors such as Natsuo Kirino and Keigo Hagashino.

Genre fiction translated from Chinese is still much less common. He Jiahong's *Black Holes*, a Chinese legal whodunit in English translation, is an almost unique entry in its small sub-genre.

Black Holes tells the story of criminal lawyer Hong Jun defending a young equities trader from a charge of fraud. Nothing is as simple as it seems, of course, and the roots of the case lie back in the Cultural Revolution. The sections of the backstory about the life of "educated youth" sent to the countryside—Heilongjiang—during the Cultural Revolution are detailed and readable, if not necessarily revelatory.

Readers of crime fiction will on the whole find themselves on familiar ground: lawyers, plot-twists, break-ins and love (requited and otherwise), long-held secrets and a car-chase. The interest is the cultural specifics: the actual court case is over very quickly, in a matter of hours, few witnesses are called, little in the way of evidence is submitted or analysed and there is no jury.

He—himself a legal expert and professor in China—also has two of the protagonists receiving their university education in the United States, and sets a good part of the book there. Since the book was originally written in Chinese for Chinese audiences, this provides Western readers a glimpse of the America through Chinese eyes, and emphasizes the role that the West plays in an increasingly large number of Chinese lives. The non-Chinese reader might discern a certain soft-pedalling on questions of judicial independence, police behavior and defendants' rights.

Black Holes, rendered into smooth English prose by Emily Jones, recognizable and in a familiar genre, provides interesting glimpses into China's development of modern institutions and popular entertainment.

On its own merits alone, though, *Black Holes* leaves something to be desired. The plot relies on coincidence and people (even former lovers) not recognizing each other, and the backstory is related in flashback rather than revealed. The characters are inconsistently developed; it can be hard to draw lines of motivations for their actions. The final disappointment is that the book seems to be set in 1999, and hence even lacks immediacy: fifteen years is a lifetime in China.

Black Holes is therefore more likely to be appreciated for its uniqueness than as an exemplar of the genre. John Grisham doesn't have much to fear from China, at least not yet.

Nevertheless, it's important that the English-speaking world have access to Chinese genre fiction as well as its literature: one learns different things. And *Black Holes*, true to its genre, will do nicely to pass the hours in a plane or airport: if one wants a Chinese whodunit, there aren't many alternatives.

Black Holes, He Jiahong (Penguin Australia, September 2014)

From the Old Country: Stories and Sketches of China and Taiwan by Zhong Lihe, edited and translated by TM McClellan

reviewed by John Butler

27 October 2014 — In 1976, there appeared in Taiwan a publication of the *Complete Works* of one Zhong Lihe, and in 1980 a biopic about this author, *China: My Native Land*, was screened. Zhong Lihe (1915-1960) was well-known in Taiwan for having produced one book of short stories during his lifetime, *Oleander* (1945), and for posthumously winning a literary prize for an unfinished novel, *Songs of Bamboo Hat Hill.* A new and revised edition of his *Complete Works* was issued in 2009.

His name, it seems, remained almost completely unknown to Western readers. Indeed, the literature of Taiwan in general receives little attention, although there is a large and flourishing community of writers there, especially short story writers, and it is to this genre that the present book belongs. Columbia University Press is to be highly commended for publishing this book (which, incidentally, includes a foreword by the author's late son) as well as an entire series of modern Chinese literature from Taiwan; it's high time that the "other" China received its due on the literary stage, and after reading this book a reviewer may well ask why it had not been translated and published years before.

Zhong Lihe came from a rural area in the southern part of Taiwan, where his father ran a farm in a small town called Meinong in the Hakka district. The Hakka people were originally immigrants from Guangdong, and are now the second-largest ethnic group in modern Taiwan.

Zhong would spend most of his life in rural communities, although he travelled to Beijing and other mainland cities, as well as spending some time in Manchuria when it was the Empire of Manchukuo, nominally presided over by the ex-emperor of China, Pu Yi, but effectively ruled as a province of Japan. Taiwan itself, of course, had been under Japanese rule since 1895.

Zhong's origins as well as his travels allowed him to form a unique perspective which is reflected in these stories, which range from local recollection and semi-fictionalised autobiography to "The Fourth Day", featuring a full cast of angry yet pitiful (and, to a degree, pitiable) Japanese soldiers (the only Japanese in the book) who prove completely unable to handle their defeat in 1945, and feel betrayed. Zhong's portrayal of these soldiers is not bitter, and the narrator almost sympathizes with their frustration and sorrow as they face the fact that the Imperial Japanese army is not, after all, invincible, and that the cause they fought for is lost. This powerful story is arguably the most moving one in the book.

* * *

Zhong's stories recreate the pre-war world of the Hakka peasantry and paint a vivid, if somewhat melancholy, picture of a world that sometimes seems to have an aura of innocence about it, but which will soon be destroyed by war and oppression, never to rise again in its original form, as the later stories show us.

Zhong's writing exhibits a certain amount of almost sentimental nostalgia for the world that has been lost; the first story in the book "My Grandma from the Mountains", looks back affectionately at an old woman who "never told lies to us children," and "always seemed to be smiling a profound, almost imperceptible smile." Hatred, falsehood and violence are in the future; the narrator doesn't even know that his grandmother is a "Gari", an aboriginal, and the Japanese don't start playing a part in his life until he goes to a Japanese school.

The stories range from the autobiographical to the more general and universal, and are divided into five parts which roughly correspond to periods in the author's life. We begin in Zhong's village, his "formative years" as he calls them, and then move out into the larger world. Zhong creates an autobiographical *persona*, A-He, but whilst he continues narrating the fictional autobiography in the second part of the book, his name is not mentioned there. Part Three returns the narrative to "The Homeland", and the last two sections are set in Meinong, where the author eventually settled.

The divisions all refer to places, which are of paramount significance to Zhong and sometimes even appear to transcend the importance of the human characters in the stories, although this is less apparent in the early childhood stories of the first part of the book, where persons, not places, seem sometimes more vivid. However, Zhong is, for the most part, equally good at evoking people; if Grandma in the opening story is just another old woman to the reader at first, by the end Zhong has brought out what made her more than that to the narrator.

He is able to do this with all the characters he presents in the various stories; Koreans, Japanese and Chinese are featured, all seen participating in the human comedy, regardless of customs, religions or nationalities. "In the Willow Shade" introduces two Koreans, Park and Kim (perhaps generic representations because these are such widespread names in Korea) who are caught up in their own social system, which dictates that they enter into arranged marriages at an early age. The narrator befriends both of them, but he is closer to Park, who, like himself, reads serious literature, and is separated from the girl he has loved since childhood; Kim, the poorer of the two, leaves school because his wife and child are practically starving. When Park leaves school to find his sweetheart, the narrator understands his decision emotionally, but cannot quite understand why his friend would throw away an education and the possibility of a good job.

For the narrator, the consideration of the practical side trumps the emotional; it's no accident that the last section of the book is entitled "Meining Economics", and in a story entitled "Rain", a "good match" is defined this way:

> he's clever, educated and has a good job. And the family, they have money, they have land, they have shops ... Your family and theirs are perfectly matched.

Zhong's narrator reveals himself as being, at heart, the practical Taiwanese who must make the correct choices; he may not understand other peoples' motivations, but he can only see them in terms of his own perspective, namely the prospective groom's earning potential and the solid wealth of his family.

The narrative has a great range, from insalubrious areas of Beijing (still called "Peking" here), rural Taiwan and Manchuria, and Zhong draws his characters from all classes and all walks of life.

This book gives readers a glance into a world that is now largely gone, completely overtaken by the modern world, where the social systems are undergoing rapid changes to a more "western" way of life.

Zhong does not judge; the narrative presents the situations from the point of view of someone caught between the two worlds, a traveller who really cannot quite come home again. This is a valuable book; it's well-translated into good idiomatic English by TM McClellan and presents a moving, living picture through its vignettes of Taiwanese life in particular, perhaps without too much nostalgia for the old ways but without entirely welcoming the new ways either.

The book is attractively illustrated, too, which contributes significantly to the immediacy of the stories. I hope that Columbia University Press will see fit to publish more of Zhong's work.

From the Old Country: Stories and Sketches of China and Taiwan, Lihe Zhong, TM McClellan (trans.), Tiejun Zhong (foreword) (Columbia University Press, February 2014)

The Unbearable Dreamworld of Champa the Driver by Chan Koonchung

reviewed by John W. W. Zeiser

20 September 2014 — In an interview with *The New York Times*, Chan Koonchung stated that "my ambition was to write an antiromantic novel about Tibet." In *The Unbearable Dreamworld of Champa the Driver* he gives us the decidedly anti-heroic Champa, whose strange quest from Lhasa to Beijing highlights the tensions facing modern Tibet. Champa isn't, as Koonchung described in that same interview, "deep. He's deeply flawed." Much the same could be said of the novel, which is at times deeply entertaining, but simultaneously lacking in depth or nuance.

Champa is a young Tibetan man who likes to drink, sleep with women, including his art-dealing Chinese boss, Plum, and—especially—he loves driving. When he got his license his "dad said: 'Now you can drive your mum and dad to Beijing.'" Something that never actually happened, but to his family, beginning with his grandfather, Beijing occupies a special place. Champa too gets the Beijing bug: "My mates at school called me 'Beijing-fixated'. I strolled along Beijing Road, watched the Beijing Olympics on TV and ate Peking Duck."

When Plum finally takes her "Champie" to the Chinese capital, he can hardly contain his excitement: "I would get to go to Beijing at last! I was thrilled... I'd imagined that, after so long, she'd come to meet me inside the terminal, and we'd throw our arms around each other. Like in the movies." Champa's expectations are too big not to fail.

Kept sequestered in a five-star hotel and shuttled from one tourist attraction to another, Plum seems to be embarrassed to be "keeping" a Tibetan, which is not the case back in Lhasa. His outing to the mythic center of China turns out to be a disappointment. To make matters worse, on the road back to Lhasa, across the Qinghai-Tibet highway, in the brand new white Range Rover Plum has given him, Champa realizes he's no longer attracted to her.

This is manifested, quite literally, in Champa's inability to get it up for Plum, except by means of imagining someone else. In a strange turn, his entire libido is caught up in a Tara statue that Plum claims looks like her, but actually resembles her daughter, Shell: "I thought of the Tara, then of Shell. Shell, Tara, Tara, Shell. The Tara merged into Shell and I wasn't thinking of the Tara any more, only of Shell."

Caught in his own mind, worrying that Plum will notice his enervated vigor, the sexually frustrated Champa fears hurting Plum's feelings, if not her safety, as one of two unsettling scenes that borders on rape displays. He has also grown attached to the material possessions and status his association with Plum provides. What's "a tough guy, a Tibetan mastiff, a heart throb" to do?

Champa decides to drive back across the Qinghai-Tibet highway to present Shell the Tara statue and be embraced by "China's mega-megalopolis". His drive east is a bit of a mini-Odyssey with strange omens and a sage hitchhiker named Nyima who has "started to do nothing" since 2008, a reference to the demonstrations in the Tibetan Autonomous Region in March of that year. Nyima keeps Champa occupied with discussions of Freud's theories of the death wish and sex-urge, Nirvana, the history of Tibet, and old Italian cinema. If there is a character in the novel that could use a dose of Freud, it is Champa.

Predictably, upon arrival in Beijing, things are much different than the movies or propaganda make it seem. Beijingers live in cramped apartments, suggest Champa work at a Tibetan restaurant, and much to his chagrin, use public transportation.

This mundane Beijing is introduced in one of the better passages of the novel, composed of nothing but text messages and tweets by animal rights activists trying to stop a truck full of stolen dogs from being taken to Jilin and used as meat. There is humor in the scene and shows off Chan's strength in utilizing the language of the digital. But there is also something revealing about how prone digital democracy can be to digression.

Shell proves to be no stabilizing force for the wayward Champa. She is literally a mess: "she couldn't even keep her things under control. Stuff was strewn around as if she was a street vendor." Champa is frustrated also by Shell's sexual confusion and ends up forcing himself on her at one point, just as he did with her mom. Although, this is meant as a metaphor for the complex relationship between China and Tibet, it reads more like an unconscious revenge fantasy and leaves one feeling quite disturbed.

This extremity draws attention to Chan's insistence that the characters be little more than ciphers. As literary inventions their motivations remain inchoate and unnuanced in the service of unmistakably delineating the novel as an allegory of Sino-Tibetan relationships. This is despite the fact that Chan didn't want to write an overly political novel of Tibet.

However, Champa is caught between Lhasa and Beijing, between modernity and history. His journey embodies the push and pull world through which Tibet wades even though Champa himself has few political leanings of his own. At most, what he finds troubling is that he and his fellow Tibetans are so restricted geographically. He sees freedom as conferred through the awarding of passports, identification cards, bribes, and the ability to drive unhindered through the cavernous expanses of China.

William Gibson once said "science fiction's best use today is the exploration of contemporary reality rather than any attempt to predict where we are going." Chan's first novel, *The Fat Years*, which was banned in China, was science fiction, but with *The Unbearable Dreamworld* he has relocated to this new tradition, underscoring the strangeness of the present rather than searching for any clues to the future. Chan's vision in combining the language of rapidly changing consumer technologies, imported red wines and luxury cars with the vast emptiness of the Qinghai-Tibet Highway remains the strongest feature of the novel. But perhaps the knowledge that such a controversial topic would never be published in China gave Chan the license to stray occasionally into the obvious.

The Unbearable Dreamworld of Champa the Driver, Chan Koonchung, Nicky Harman (trans.) (Transworld Publishers Ltd, May 2014)

The Ten Thousand Things by John Spurling

reviewed by Jonathan Chatwin

7 September 2014 — John Spurling's fictionalized life of Wang Meng, one of the four artistic masters of the Yuan dynasty, begins with the artist languishing in prison, finally subject to the forces of the complex political world he spent much of his life eschewing. Declaring life to be "much simpler than one imagines to start with"—it is merely a question of following one's nature, he asserts—the seventy-eight year old Wang goes on to recount a personal narrative marked by complexity and profound existential uncertainty. The seeming contradiction is characteristic of Wang, who—after his years of willful isolation and intense artistic pursuit—has comes to understand his craft, but not himself.

Certainty of self, however, is perhaps an not an overtly desirable asset in Wang's lifetime; with the Mongol Yuan dynasty beginning to crumble and bandits roaming the country, declaring oneself too certainly is a dangerous act, particularly for an individual such as Wang, a minor and reluctant official who is descended from the line of the Song dynasty emperors. Wang's uncalculated mutability and calculated reticence generally manages to keep him from falling into the trouble that affects many of those around him.

Spurling is a scholar of art history, and his erudition and understanding are evident in his masterful characterization of Wang. Contemporary, yet of his time; complex, but never self-consciously or distractingly so, he is a creation reminiscent, in the subtlety and sophistication of his development, of Thomas Cromwell in Hilary Mantel's garlanded *Wolf Hall* and *Bring up the Bodies*. Historical fiction is all too often a lowest-common-denominator pursuit, in which little care is expended in developing characters beyond stereotypes. In *The Ten Thousand Things*, Wang seems never less than a cohesive fictional protagonist, whilst also manifesting a fragile and compelling humanity.

As a young man, Wang is pulled unwillingly from the pastoral retreat he has established beneath the Yellow Crane Mountain. Rebels arrive at his house, accidentally burning down his studio and killing his servant. Wang feels a compulsion to follow and assist these bandits, who are led by a vengeful but beautiful woman named the White Tigress, and for whom he devises a strategy to enable them to exact revenge on a magistrate responsible for the death of their kin. From here, Wang seems set to play a prominent role in the rebellion against the Yuan; yet, with the White Tigress killed in the battle he has orchestrated, Wang returns to his wife and the Yellow Crane Mountain, content to remain, for a time at least, on the periphery.

The Ten Thousand Things is a fundamentally undramatic novel—something which comes as a surprise, given Spurling's background as a playwright and the tumultuous times in which the work is set. The narrative is essentially anticlimactic, partly as a consequence of the material facts of Wang's biography, to which Spurling is largely faithful, but also because his central protagonist is so profoundly concerned with the artistic imperative of maintaining an appropriate distance between himself and the world—a distance which, given Wang's somewhat changeable nature, narrows and widens over the course of the novel, but which is never entirely closed.

However, the novel's narrative approach also seems to owe something to both classical Chinese literature and Wang's own artistic style, with the Aristotelian dramatic paradigm consciously ignored in favor of a model which impassively delineates the intricate detail of a life lived in interesting times. Spurling's approach feels perfectly attuned to his subject, and one can pay no higher compliment than to say that on finishing the novel it is hard to believe that the work is anything other than the lost manuscript of the great Wang Meng himself.

Ten Thousand Things, John Spurling (Overlook Duckworth, April 2014; Overlook Duckworth, April 2014)

I Am China by Guo Xiaolu

reviewed by Loh Su Hsing

9 August 2014 — The latest novel from prolific writer Guo Xiaolu is an ambitious endeavor. At 370 pages, this is Guo's longest work of fiction to date, and by her own admission in an interview, "the most demanding and slowest project I've worked on so far." And it is easy to see why—Guo has taken on love, exile, translation, Chinese politics, art and attempted to interweave these themes into a story mostly related in an epistolary style.

Iona is a Scottish translator who has been tasked by a publishing house in London to translate a set of documents related to a famous Chinese musician, which might potentially be published into a book. These turn out to be a series of diary entries and letters exchanged between Kublai Jian, a Chinese-Mongol punk musician who is in exile in Europe due to his political beliefs, and his girlfriend, Mu.

As Iona pieces together the story of Jian and Mu, she finds herself drawn towards their struggle and grows increasingly retrospective of her own unsatisfactory life. She ultimately decides to try to reunite Jian and Mu, but fails to avert an imminent tragedy.

While Guo's observations about Chinese politics and art come across as emphatic and heartfelt, the narrative sometimes borders on the implausible and melodramatic—Jian writes to the Queen to seek political asylum and gets a reply stating

> one believes you will manage to gain solid ground through the legal process... We listened with some degree of interest to this assemblage of undoubtedly authentic ethnic expression. Indeed, we were amused. We

> believe your musical career will continue to flourish despite your current difficulties...

Iona is late by a day in preventing Jian's suicide in Crete; the head of the publishing house, Jonathan, finds out that his wife eloped with her yoga instructor to India; Jian's father turns out to be the incumbent prime minister of China who abandoned his young son in order to further his political career.

Guo is most articulate when writing on China and it is tempting to draw parallels between the novel and her own life—like the protagonist, Mu, Guo's mother sang in a travelling troupe, her father was a painter who suffered for his art during the Cultural Revolution, she was raised in a village by her grandparents, and her parents passed away from cancer; and like the other protagonist Jian, Guo sought asylum in Britain. The seemingly problematic—in her view—dichotomy between East and West, an oft-repeated theme in her books, is again at play in this novel, though somewhat less nuanced.

> The Westerner, the white Caucasian of Europe, is superior, and the Western woman is the untouchable one—she is the top prize in the world of sexual conquest...

It is not unusual for writers to write in a second language—Conrad, Kerouac and Beckett being but a few prominent examples—but this seems to inhibit Guo in this particular novel compared to her previous work. Her observations in the book on translating between English and Chinese

> There are so many basic difficulties in translating Chinese into English, Iona thinks. No tense differentiation; no conjugation of verbs; no articles, no inversion in questions—and I have to invent all this and add it to fit the translation... The Roman letters of English and the oriental characters of Chinese are not natural bedfellows.

appear to manifest themselves in sometimes inconsistent prose and awkward similes:

> Iona has an image of two revolutionaries in love. Their strong emotions colour her mind with shades of red and shimmering blue.
>
> She stops at the central point, sees the city crouching on both sides of the great gash of river whose waves spread wide the legs of the capital.

I am China was published on Tiananmen's 25th anniversary and the greatest strengths of the book, indeed, are Guo's acute observations on the emotional and intellectual aftermath of the massacre. She vividly captures the mixed emotions of the youths of 1980s about their home country and the impact on their lives decades after. These parts of the narrative are a compelling read. However, Guo's bold attempt in probing and integrating complex themes just might have attenuated the essence of what she has described as her final piece of work on her homeland and "her goodbye love letter to China."

I am China, Xiaolu Guo (Vintage, June 2014; Nan A. Talese, September 2014)

Night in Shanghai by Nicole Mones

reviewed by Agnès Bun

11 July 2014 — There is a tragic beauty in cities on the verge of collapsing.

The First World War had left the world on its knees; the Roaring Twenties were the answer to these grim years, with people frantically dancing ghastly memories away in European ballrooms.

Shanghai, heavy with foreign presence, also dazzled in the interwar years. However in this city, largely undisturbed by the depression gripping Europe, the good times extended for another decade. Clubs shone with the glow of post-battle adrenaline. There was in the air the feeling that everything is possible, even something as peculiar as jazz in China.

But war was about to trip the world up again.

Night in Shanghai is set in just this place and just this time. The novel is populated by such colorful characters as Thomas Green, an African-American from Baltimore, "caramel-toned, with eyes as dark as ink", who has come to Shanghai to front a jazz band: "Shanghai! It was alluring, dangerous; there were songs about it." Then there is Lin, the romantic bastard of a triad lord, and Song, a fierce modern Mulan whose freedom had been sold to repay her father's gambling debts. Their fates entangle from these pre-war years until the Japanese invasion of Shanghai and its aftermath, against the dramatic backdrop of glitter and guns.

The book opens with Thomas's arrival in Shanghai. He has been invited by Lin, a Chinese admirer of jazz. The musician comes at a critical time:

> The years before the war forced everyone in Shanghai to choose: National-

ists or Communists? Resist the Japanese invaders or collaborate with them? Even passivity became a choice, a gamble, a hand consciously played.

As Thomas tries to find his place in the band he is supposed to lead and the city where he has decided to live, he is dragged against his will into the political turmoil that agitates the city. The Green Gang, a local triad, sees in him the perfect bait to reach a Japanese officer, and murder him.

But Thomas also catches the eye of a Russian socialite and—against all the odds—of Song: the American jazzman, shining on the stage of bars and concert halls, seems to have nothing in common with this Chinese communist activist, used to working in the shadows. Music suddenly becomes a pretext to kill, or to love.

American author Nicole Mones spent almost two decades in China, arriving in 1977 right after the end of the Cultural Revolution. As someone born and raised in the land of the American dream, she is well-placed to depict what the lesser-known Shanghainese dream was for the lost souls who washed up on the shores of the Pearl of the Orient. "Everyone in Shanghai had a story," she writes. "It was that kind of place."

The novel excels in its flamboyant portrayal of Shanghai as a Noah's Ark of musicians, gamblers, drug addicts, poets, triad members and prostitutes. Page after page, the multiple faces of Shanghai's nights are outlined; the worlds of the underground and entertainment tango provocatively. Triad matters are discussed behind the seemingly innocent façade of a popular jazz band; secret communist plots are devised in the quietness of a humble apothecary shop.

Behind closed doors, all these parallel universes unravel and coexist in an unstable balance, until they eventually collide. Soon the drums of war drown out the jazz notes. And Thomas's band players leave one by one, marking the slow but inexorable death of a city swallowed by the conflict between the Japanese and the Chinese forces.

Within each of Mones's characters lies an inner tragedy, an identity struggle: Thomas's skin color, Lin's social upbringing, Song's gender. For Thomas who struggled to fit in America, acceptance comes through music, and his ticket to Shanghai.

> Suddenly he wasn't different anymore, everybody was different. No one looked twice at him, for the first time in his life... He made sense in Shanghai.

Song's dream leads her to the Communists, whom she joins in order to escape from her position as a subservient female servant trapped in a patriarchal society that Mones succinctly describes: "She was only a girl with no more power than a grain of millet afloat in a vast sea."

Both are damned in the same hell, just with different devils. For Thomas, redemption eventually comes through art; for Song, through political commitment.

A strength of the book is its musical quality. Jazz—"the sun around which this paradise revolved, the rhythm that drove its nights"—in particular plays a cathartic function in a world about to fall apart.

But beyond the jazz played in its clubs, Shanghai itself is a score, a honeycomb pulsing with a unique melody described by Mones as "the chants of the vendors, the buzz of the barber's fork, the temple bells."

And as the plot carries on at its own pace, the reader is almost left breathless trying to follow its allegro rhythm. Even as the story gets darker, music remains, and Thomas continues to play, almost successful in relegating war to background noise.

Right at the beginning of *Night in Shanghai*, Mones quotes this Chinese saying: "An inch of time is worth an inch of gold, an inch of gold cannot buy an inch of time." And at the novel's center are days gone forever; it takes us through Shanghai's golden years and then through its agonizing demise.

The Japanese invasion punched a hole in the city's history; about 250,000 people died on the Chinese side, 70,000 on the Japanese. Eventually the Japanese army won and took over, irrevocably changing the face of the city: "a cruel parody of what had been." The contrast between the pre-war splendor and the post-war hungover is masterfully recreated here, with a palpably painful melancholy.

Standing up, and falling down again: there is sadness in going through these pages, watching the night fall on Shanghai. As the lights go out, everyone suddenly looks older; and all that is left is the bitter aftertaste of good times gone.

Night in Shanghai, Nicole Mones (Houghton Mifflin Harcourt, March 2014)

Song of King Gesar by Alai, translated by Howard Goldblatt and Sylvia Li-chun Lin

reviewed by Rosie Milne

13 April 2014 — The epic *The Song of Gesar* is the Tibetan equivalent, if there can be such a thing, of the Iliad or the Ramayana. Like these other national classics, it was passed down in song from one generation to the next; in what must surely be one of the last surviving examples of this ancient tradition Tibetan bards recite it even today.

Alai, a Chinese author of Tibetan descent, has incorporated the epic into a novel, set partly in ancient Tibet, where evil spirits interfered in the lives of humans, and partly in the modern day, where songs from the Gesar cycle are broadcast by Tibetan radio stations.

Many readers may feel they are reading *The Song of King Gesar* through multiple veils of ignorance: ignorance of Tibet and its history; of Buddhism; of the Chinese language. While much is strange to Western ears, the translation into English prose by Howard Goldblatt and Sylvia Li-chun Lin flows naturally.

The Song of King Gesar tells of two lives entwined, those of Gesar and of Jigmed. In mythical times, Gesar, the youngest and bravest of the gods, was sent down to the human world to defeat the demons that plagued the lives of ordinary people. Jigmed is a modern-day shepherd boy chosen by the gods to be a storyteller, and to sing of Gesar's achievements.

Indeed, *The Song of King Gesar* is an extended meditation on storytelling, and on the power of stories both in the lives of individuals, and in forging and maintaining a culture's identity. Alai repeatedly cuts from the story, the myth of Gesar, to the storyteller, Jigmed. Gesar and Jigmed commune in the world of dreams:

> There were now two Gesars in Jigmed's mind. One was the hero of the stories he sang. The other was the Gesar whose dream he'd entered, the god born into the human world. Yet though the dream was not quite real, and he could remember only blurred grey images, he preferred the Gesar of the dream.

The story sections of the book concern Gesar's victories over various adversaries, both demon and human, in struggles as diverse as battles and horse races, until he unites the people of Gling (Tibet), and brings to them an era of peace and prosperity.

> [After the demon king of Jang had been conquered] the territory, population and treasure of Gling increased many times. Intimidated by Gling's power and King Gesar's reputation, the neighbouring countries were content to live peacefully side by side and enter into trade agreements, which further increased Gling's wealth and power. Her people enjoyed a decade with no wars, and no scourge of demons. Gesar's palace was filled with rare treasures from all over the world. Temples, houses, workshops and shops rose up around the palace, like mushrooms after summer rain.

Eventually, Gesar returns to heaven, never again to come down to the world of humans, except through the dreams of poets.

Meanwhile, the storyteller sections of the book follow Jigmed's life both as a man, and as a bard. As a man, his problems are typical:

> He did not believe that he had fallen in love with the woman in the recording studio: how could two people from such different backgrounds be in love? Had her suggestive voice or wanton fragrance beguiled him? Was that why he felt drugged?

As a bard, Jigmed sings of Gesar at contemporary gatherings, such as a cherry festival.

> The town was crowded: cherry merchants, journalists and officials who outranked local officials. Even so, Jigmed was put up in a room of his own

> at a hotel, where they had laid out promotional brochures with pictures of him singing in his storytelling outfit. He was pleased. That day during the opening ceremonies he'd sung only a brief passage, barely finding his voice before applause carried him offstage, where he'd had to press himself to a wall to make way for a group of girls, made up like bright red cherries.

Ultimately, Jigmed loses his ability to sing—the Living Buddha catches the last of his song on a small tape recorder. In an example of the symbolism in which the book abounds, Jigmed's ability to sing, his communion with Gesar, is represented by an arrow in his back. This arrow sometimes seems metaphorical, and sometimes literal. As Jigmed loses the ability to sing, a literal physical arrow falls from his back.

* * *

Alai conveys a compelling sense of place; the descriptions of the Tibetan landscape—the vast grasslands, vast skies, and snow-capped mountains—are sharply detailed, and almost yearning:

> The wind blew back the grass seeds, the seeds of azaleas, giant cypresses and birch. And there were seeds of rosemary, too, with its dusty blue flowers. It took only a single night and a fine drizzle for the seeds to sprout, and on the third day, before the palisade around the tent was finished, flowers were blooming across the grassland.

The glimpses of ancient Tibetan thought are illuminating, for example the casting of moles as demons, burrowing away under the soil, destroying the link between the earth and vegetation, so: "the pasture grass reached down with its roots and grasped nothing but black emptiness." It is good for those of us living far, far from the grasslands to be reminded of the centrality of grass to life.

Likewise, the glimpses of modern Tibetan society are interesting, and the depiction of the continuing relationship between Tibetans and their horses is delightful; even in the contemporary sections, this novel about stories and storytelling features horses that can listen to, and benefit from, stories.

> [Jigmed] stood in front of the horse and smoothed its mane as he began to sing. He saw that the shadows of the willow gathered, as if they, too, were listening to him. The horse pricked its ears and its dull coat grew lustrous as Jigmed sang.

For all its pleasures, this book can in places be hard going. It can be difficult to keep all the Tibetan names straight, and those without knowledge of Tibetan Buddhism may flounder with questions about the various Bodhisattvas, or be distracted by irrelevant detail such as why Guanyin appeared sometimes to be male, and sometimes female.

But difficulties and ambiguities are surely inherent in offering an ancient national epic to a contemporary readership living beyond its homeland. *The Song of King Gesar* succeeds in promoting cultural communion; anybody interested in Tibet, or in the power of stories, should read this exhilaratingly weird book.

Song of King Gesar, Alai, Sylvia Li-Chun Lin & Howard Goldblatt (trans.) (Canongate Books Ltd, November 2013)

Children's fiction: *Three Years and Eight Months* by Icy Smith, illustrated by Jennifer Kindert

reviewed by Jane Houng

28 June 2014 — In spite of a long and varied history, to say nothing of being a city of seven-million, Hong Kong has relatively few children's books set there; even fewer deal with the dark days of the Second World War or feature the local, as opposed to expat, population. The multicultural storybook *Three Years and Eight Months* can't fill this gap on its own, but it helps. Written by award-winning Chinese-American author Icy Smith, her heart-warming story is loosely based on the true life experiences of her father and an uncle between 1942 to 1945.

The main character is a ten-year old Eurasian boy called Choi who, at the beginning of the story, hears loud sirens and sees smoke "in the distance." Then, after his mother is dragged away by Japanese soldiers, he has to hide away with an uncle. The situation improves when Choi meets another Chinese-American boy and they are befriended by a Japanese soldier called Watanabe-san who teaches them Japanese and finds them chores working as slave boys in a military station. While delivering a package, Choi discovers that his mother is working as a washerwoman nearby. Then, after reuniting with his uncle who "sees many dying and injured people every day", the boys start pilfering medical supplies from the military station. They eventually discover that they indirectly helped save "hundreds of lives" because Choi's uncle was working for an underground anti-Japanese resistance group called the East River Column.

The only remotely similar books that come to mind are Martin Booth's novel *Music on the Bamboo Radio*, in which an eleven-year old English boy disguises himself as a Chinese youngster and helps the Communist faction of the East River Column blow up Japanese infrastructure and, somewhat farther afield, JG Ballard's *Empire of the Sun*, in which an English boy finds himself in a camp in Shanghai; both have found their way on to school curricula.

Whereas both Booth's and Ballard's books are novelistic in scope and style, *Three Years and Eight Months* is written more for educational purposes. For example, it includes detailed historical notes and original photographs at the back of the book. Covering four years of personal history in first person present tense gives rise to occasional technical problems in the narrative, and Smith's style is somewhat factual and telling, but Kindert's copious illustrations will surely draw young readers into the story. Her dramatic watercolors highlight interesting local details, from trams and local buildings, local artefacts to Chinese cuisine. Japanese details abound too—a portrait of Hirohito, uniforms, flags, aircraft, warships, currency.

The explicit details of abuse and cruelty are delicately avoided in the story. For example, we learn that the Chinese women who felt shame for "socializing" with Japanese soldiers became Buddhist nuns. Similarly, Watanabe-san is portrayed with empathy—we discover that he knew the boys were stealing, and feels fearful for his personal safety when returning to Japan. These soft touches, plus the positive themes of friendship, bravery and sacrifice are well-suited for a middle grade audience.

Three Years and Eight Months, Icy Smith, Jennifer Kindert (illus.) (East West Discovery Press, May 2013)

Decoded by Mai Jia

reviewed by Melanie Ho

MAI JIA

16 June 2014 — The first of Mai Jia's books to be translated into English, *Decoded* tells the story about a mathematical genius named Rong Jinzhen, whose talent sees him recruited to Unit 701, the cryptography department in China's secret services where Jinzhen is tasked to the elusive Code Purple, the most difficult cypher the unit had been tasked to break.

At first glance, *Decoded* appears to have all of the necessary conventions of a thriller— cryptography, a mathematical genius, a code that needs breaking, key locations shrouded in secrecy (N University, B City, G Province)—but if this is a thriller, it's not a conventional one.

Before the story arrives at Unit 701, Mai Jia (the pen name for Jiang Benhu) takes the reader through the history of the Rong family starting in the 19th-century when one member, Rong Zilai, is sent to the United States and learns the art of interpreting dreams. He returns having studied mathematics and founds a school that grows into a university.

The Rongs become known for their mathematical abilities, including the talented "Abacus" Rong Youying, whose life—and brilliant career—is cut short during childbirth. Her son is sent away and it is his illegitimate son who becomes known as Rong Jinzhen. Once Jinzhen is integrated into the Rong family and his mathematical genius is uncovered, he begins to study under Jan Lesiewicz, a professor at the university.

The relationship between Rong Jinzhen and Lesiewicz—himself also a mathematical genius—is at the heart of the narrative and Mai Jia explores their bond, which comes into play later in the story. It is also an opportunity for a discussion on mathematical history, adding another layer of complexity, some of which foreshadows later events and others which seems to add to the book's philosophical level:

> Calculation often proves a slipshod method of determining the future—it shows the possible as being impossible. People often do no work as tidily as calculations: they can make the impossible possible; they can turn earth into heavens. That means that in actual fact there is no great gulf between heaven and earth: one fraction more and earth becomes heaven, one fraction less and heaven will change into earth.

A "semi-autistic" (as the book jacket describes him) mathematical genius, known to his classmates as an idiot-savant, it is Rong Jinzhen's ability to see connections where others cannot that help him in his attempt to solve Code Purple.

> As we know, Jinzhen treated other people with an unusual degree of coldness—he liked spending time on his own. He had very little experience of interacting with his peers. This was a weak point in his character and something that would endanger him greatly in the future.

The narrative is interspersed by transcripts of interviews that the narrator has conducted with people in Rong Jinzhwen's life. The interviews help create a closeness to Rong, but also to illuminate and provide context to the series of events in his life. They also help push the story along and Mai does well to give each interviewee a distinct voice. As the narrator explores Rong Jinzhwen's early life at the university's mathematics department, he discovers that Rong was the only student permitted to borrow Professor Liseiwicz's books. An interview with Master Rong reveals:

> The problem is that the blanket ban applied to everyone except Zhendi, and so people started making wild guesses about what was going on. There were all sorts of stories circulating in the mathematics department anyway about what a genius Zhendi was—how he completed four years of study in the space of two weeks, how cold sweat broke out on Professor Liseiwicz's face at the mere sight of him; and before you knew it, some people who didn't understand the first thing about how these things work were saying

that the foreign professor was using Zhendi's intelligence to advance his own research.

Mai seems to have drawn on his life for at least certain elements of the book: Mai kept a diary (of which there are 36 volumes) and served 17 years in the army, where he specialized in cryptography; the editorial letter describes him "[remaining] something of an enigma" despite his books' popularity in China.

There is very little description of the actual code breaking and the first 100 pages are dedicated to the, albeit fascinating, story of the Rong family and the mystery is more a journey into the mind of a mathematical genius. This is not to say that the book is not intriguing—Mai Jia weaves in discussions of mathematical history and philosophy and human suffering into the code-breaking plot—but the spy/thriller element seems to be more of a conduit for Mai Jia to delve into the mind of Rong Jinzhen rather than a straight whodunit. It's a slow burn, but a mystery all the better for it.

Decoded; A Novel, Mai Jia (Penguin Books Ltd, March 2014; Farrar Strauss Giroux, March 2014)

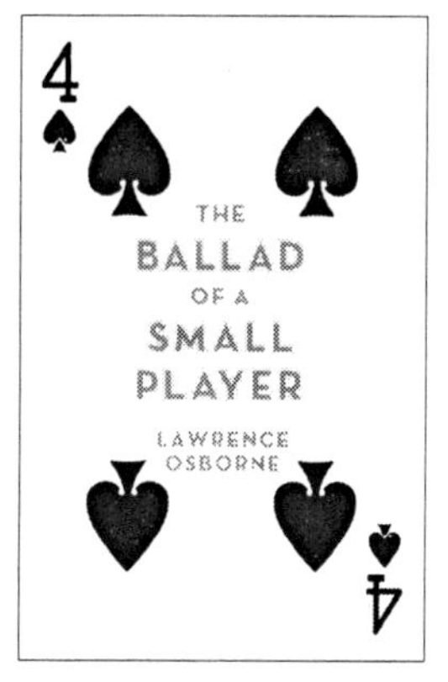

The Ballad of a Small Player by Lawrence Osborne

reviewed by Peter Gordon

28 May 2014 — There is nothing in the title or on the stylish cover of (at least the British edition of) Lawrence Osborne's slim new novel to indicate that the book is set entirely in Macau and Hong Kong. While an admirable breach of marketing convention, this means it may also slip unnoticed by many potential readers in what must surely be a key market.

That would be a great shame, for *The Ballad of a Small Player* is one of the best, and quite possibly the best, East Asian "expat novel" of the past decade. I realize with concern that this may come across as damning with faint praise.

The often pejorative "expat fiction"—applied to novels written by, in the main, white visitors to Asia—needn't necessarily be a term of disdain, for the genre includes such writers as Somerset Maugham, Shirley Hazzard, Graham Greene, Paul Theroux and JG Ballard. There is no reason why Hong Kong and its sister city of Macau should not make for as great English-language fiction as such other foreign locales as Berlin or Paris, but despite—or perhaps because of—the Asian cities' obvious attractions, lightning of the literary kind rarely seems to strike. The results are usually dreary and formulaic processions of bar girls, fast money, deadbeat caucasian males, drugs and crooks.

These elements form the basis of *The Ballad of a Small Player* too, but Osborne—against the odds, one has to say—pulls off a virtuoso performance that isn't, in the end, about any of those things.

The phoney Lord Doyle, in actuality a crooked lawyer who embezzled a suitcaseful of money and scarpered to Asia, is gambling his way through his ill-gotten fortune in the casinos of Macau. His game of choice is baccarat punto blanco—"the slutty dirty queen of card games"—governed by pure luck. A score of nine, a "natural", is the highest possible score.

Doyle has ups and downs, more downs than ups, and along with girls, drink and fancy meals, the money is dwindling. Doyle, in spite of his yellow kid gloves and smart suits, seems to be playing himself into deliberate oblivion. Doyle isn't very likeable, even when he is.

Then he meets Dao-Ming, one of the girls that frequent such places, and his luck changes. Dao-Ming, of course, is not quite what she appears to be.

To say more, would spoil the plot. But suffice it to say that *The Ballad of a Small Player* is much more *La Pique Dame*—at least the Tchaikovsky version I know if not the Pushkin I don't—than *Suzie Wong* and as such, the setting adds color and verisimilitude without becoming the point of the book.

What sets the novel apart is not so much the plotting or characterization, but the writing: the elegant prose, the changes of pace, the crisp dialogue and the descriptions that transport the reader into the scene.

> She perched at the far end of the table with a vulgar little handbag of the kind you can buy in Shenzhen, badly made Fendi with gilt metal that flakes away a week, and her left hand rested protectively on a small pile of lower-denomination red chips...
>
> She was saying thank you or some such thing, and her lips moved like two parallel fingers playing a game of rock-paper-scissors.

Chips come "in a great salacious pile", "glass screens are frosted with images of Confucius and naked girls" and as Doyle sees himself through another's eyes, having "the look of an New England literature professor out on town without permission from his wife". When he drinks, it is not generically red but "Lello Douro", the buffet sports *oeufs savoyards*, he frequents the very real Fernando's, Robuchon and Pasteleria Koi Kei.

Those who don't live in East Asia might read *The Ballad of a Small Player* for the exoticism of its locales and the descriptions of the extravagant seediness of the Macau casinos.

Those who live here know all this, of course. Some will read it voyeuristically no doubt, but others will be transfixed by the way Osborne has turned our corner of the world, and all those things that make it what it is, from humidity to egg tarts and gaudy statues in casino lobbies, into a story that reaches well beyond it.

Any "old China hand" thinking of turning his (or these days, her) hand to semi-autobiographical fiction would do well to read this first.

Anyone else would do well to read it too.

The Ballad of a Small Player, Lawrence Osborne (Hogarth, April 2014)

Mu Shiying: China's Lost Modernist: New Translations and an Appreciation by Andrew David Field

reviewed by John Butler

26 May 2014 — "Shanghai. A heaven built upon a hell!" These simple and striking words from a Chinese writer almost completely unknown to Western readers, sum up the theme of the stories in this slim volume which introduces us to one of China's first "modernist" writers, Mu Shiying (1912-1940) and his world, the Shanghai of the 1930s, uneasily making its own way along a path between old Chinese Confucian traditions and the lure of Western culture, fashion and attitudes.

Its people are divided; on the one hand there are those who find themselves in a state which Mu describes as "No sorrows, and no joys—an emotional vacuum. Yet, then where to go?" and those on the other side, partying as if there is no tomorrow. Behind this lies the grim underbelly of Shanghai, where people can be easily disposed of in back alleys: "*Bang!* The hand lets go, the man falls down, clutching his stomach. *Bang!* Another shot... 'See you again next life, pal.'"

And then there are the women, available or pretending to be available, teasing, alluring and manipulative. They seem to dance endlessly in the smoky nightclubs, moving erotically to the sound of American jazz, enjoying the power they have over the men; one of the dancers, for example, describes herself as a "peony spirit", something from Chinese legend, where the peony represents riches and honor. "How do you know that she is a Peony Spirit?" asks the narrator of "Black Peony", and receives the answer "She told me the next day, every day upon waking, she goes and waters that black peony..."

Mu Shiying was born in the year of the abdication of China's last emperor, Pu Yi, and came of age just when that same last emperor was made the first emperor of Manchukuo by the Japanese. This places him in a period of Chinese history that is perhaps not so well-known as either that of the Manchu or Qing Dynasties which immediately preceded it or the Communist period which followed it.

It was a time when Shanghai was, as Andrew Field points out in his lengthy and indispensable introduction to this book, "infamous for its outrageous blend of Chinese and Western modernities." On one side of the road you could enter the mysterious world of Chinese opera, and then go across the same road and watch a film starring Hollywood actors like Norma Shearer and Nancy Carroll, to name two mentioned by Mu.

There were cars everywhere, but also rickshaws, and neon lights blazed alongside flickering Chinese lanterns. It was a heady mix then, and the people of Shanghai took to it with gusto, as did the young Mu Shiying, who moved there in the early 1930s from Zhejiang province to pursue a career as a writer and journalist. Ten years later he suffered the fate of the man described above, falling victim to what looked like an arranged assassination for his involvement in the Chinese peace movement and his earlier favoring collaboration with the Japanese after fighting in Shanghai broke out in 1932.

Andrew Field has selected the stories presented here from Mu's second collection, published in 1933 and entitled *Public Cemetery*. "In my society," Mu writes in his introduction to this book, "are those who have been crushed flat by life and those who have been squeezed out by life," but he goes on to explain that this does not necessarily make them angry, bitter or even tragic.

In these stories Mu features, for the most part, male narrators who have found themselves entangled romantically with the singers and dancers in Shanghai cabarets. This was a world Mu knew quite a lot about, as he himself had married a cabaret dancer; he sees the nightclubs and cabarets as a microcosm of the new attitudes sweeping Shanghai and perhaps much of the rest of China as well, which have fostered alienation and uncertainty as they ate away at the old values and customs of Chinese civilisation. Women were breaking out of their old roles, and now relationships between unmarried women and men were becoming the norm rather than the exception.

In the stories, whether Mu intended it this way or not, it seems that the patriarchal society has broken down and that the men are no longer certain of themselves; Mu's women are unpredictable and the relationships the men form with them are often volatile, unstable and confusing. In "The Man Who Was Treated as a Plaything", for example, we have two young students who meet at university and whose relationship develops into something, but the reader never knows just what its nature is. Rongzhi, the woman, is not faithful to her would-be lover, and it drives him crazy. At one point he is out boating and sees her in a boat with another man; when Rongzhi sees him, she jumps into his boat, which confuses him completely. She is a sexually-liberated woman who has rejected all the Confucian values of chastity and obedience; he cannot deal with this and ends up telling himself (in the form of a song as he looks over the Huangpu river) "I am a plaything after all!" and decides, rather enigmatically, that "A lonely man ought to simply buy a cane."

Mu employs a style of writing that is both realistic in detail and yet sometimes verging on what in the West literary critics might call "stream-of-consciousness". It is this hybrid style which distinguishes him from other Chinese writers, particularly those of the so-called "realist" school and others who were more ideologically-driven.

Mu was never an ideologue, but a true "modernist", a writer who found what he wanted in the seamier side of Shanghai life, peopling his stories with frustrated lovers who were engaged in a never-ending struggle within the confines of the urban space and using the evocation of the sensuality of individual men and women to depict that space.

Some of the stories reminded me of James Joyce's *Dubliners* (1914) with its litany of sad people, and sometimes even of *Ulysses* with Mu's fragmented dialogue, although the spaces in Mu's stories are perhaps smaller and there is little interior monologue. Like Joyce's depiction of Dublin, Mu's daring and gritty portrait of raw Shanghai life in the early 1930's was indeed something new at the time, and the "Five people beaten by life" in the story entitled "Five in a Nightclub" are perhaps the most Joycean of the characters who appear in this book. I use the comparison with Joyce merely to contextualize for Western readers. Mu was familiar with some Western writers, but his main influences, at least as he tells us, were not Joyce or any English writers, but the French short-story writer Paul Morand, who wrote of Paris and New York, and the Japanese Yokomitsu Riichi, whose novel *Shanghai*, published in series between 1928 and 1930, depicts the life of Japanese expatriates against the turbulent background of Mu's own city at the same time Mu was working on *Public Cemetery*.

Mu's stories give readers a glimpse into the lively and vibrant, yet sometimes empty and soulless life in Shanghai during the early 1930s. Nightclub life, one suspects, has not changed much, although the music accompanying has, and the whole scene as depicted by Mu has a melancholy and pointlessness brooding over it which illustrates the two sides of cosmopolitan life, and not just that in Republican China.

Underneath the surface can be found social criticism and a wider concern with the human condition; Mu never allows his creative eye to be distracted from the human in order to indulge a didactic or preachy "socialist" view of the world. Indeed, it almost seems that his characters' oppression comes from within themselves, not from European or Japanese imperialists or profiteering Chinese capitalists. In "Night", as the drunkard shouts "I'm going back home, back home, back home!," the girl in the black Chinese gown, whose name we find out only on the last page of the story, "sighed quietly" and said "We are all homeless people!" The narrator spends the night with the girl and wonders, just for a moment, whether she's the one, but as they part the reader is left to wonder, too. Another bar, another cigarette (a prominent motif in Mu's stories), another bed, another lover, and the cycle begins again.

Mu Shiying: China's Lost Modernist: New Translations and an Appreciation, Andrew Field (Hong Kong University Press, January 2014)

Snow and Shadow by Dorothy Tse, translated by Nicky Harman

reviewed by Peter Gordon

30 March 2014 — Rudyard Kipling's famous maxim that "East is East and West is West, and never the twain shall meet" might have been written specifically to describe Hong Kong's writing scene.

If I were to ask English-language readers to name a Hong Kong writer, I am certain that almost everyone, especially when it came to prose, would come up blank. Timothy Mo left town decades ago; Martin Booth, Christopher New and John Lanchester may have lived here for some time, but are—or were—arguably part of an international English-language mainstream. Those who follow such things may know of Leung Ping-kwan, who managed better than perhaps anyone else to bridge the Chinese-English divide; he however was a poet.

There are course Hong Kong writers who publish in Chinese, but these are—I think it is fair to say—largely unknown outside Chinese literary circles. One can pick out Dung Kai-Cheung, author of *Atlas: The Archaeology of an Imaginary City* and Chan Koonchung, author of *Fat Years*. Still, for a city of seven million, that's not many who are accessible to English-language readers.

Hong Kong publisher Muse is, therefore, to be commended for bringing out Dorothy Tse's short story collection *Snow and Shadow*. And not just bring it out, one has to add, but in an elegant edition. Tse is a winner of the Hong Kong Award for Chinese Literature as well several literary awards in Hong Kong and Taiwan.

These stories "are not for the faint-hearted", writes translator Nicky Harman's in her introduction, a comment reprised by Leo Ou-fan Lee on the back cover. Indeed, they are not: "limbs, and even heads," Harman goes on, "are lopped off with alarming regularity."

Nor are they easy reads. Most employ a heavy dose of the surreal or, perhaps, an extremely warped version of a city that is recognizable, albeit barely, as Hong Kong. Characters are referred to as letters or are given evocative names like "Flower", "Tree" and "Wood". The stories may start normally

> Neither of them remembered exactly when things went wrong. But at some point Knife began to cough.

but slowly or abruptly enter a dreamlike state or go completely off the rails. Some stories start off that way:

> When Flower got up that morning, Tree's head had vanished.
>
> She got a bamboo clothes pole and poked around under the bed and in the cracks in the walls, opened every drawer one by one, and searched through the cans of KK chocolate creams and cream twists. (Her son had once said he liked the brand.) But there was no sign of Tree's head.

Tse furthermore has something of an obsession with insects and, well, vermin which appear in one role or another in most of the stories.

This is a collection that is, in sum, uncomfortable, weird and disturbing, requiring close reading but which can also prove thought-provoking. It is not immediately clear, nor indeed is it clear after some considerable reflection, exactly what Tse is up to. What may be most surprising for English-language readers—for whom Hong Kong has seemed a rather placid place—is the undercurrent of, if not anger then, as Harman quotes the author in her useful and entirely necessary introduction, "resistance". Tse goes on: "In Hong Kong, writing is itself an active rejection of utilitarian society and mundane everyday life."

"Surrealism," writes Harman, "occupies a special place in Hong Kong writing." From the small sample of Hong Chinese literature in translation I have access to, that—without dwelling too much on the exact literary definition of surrealism—seems to be the case. Dung Kai-Cheung's *Atlas* is also a rather strange book, a novel largely without plot or even characters.

Snow and Shadow would seem to confirm that Chinese- and English-language writing from Hong Kong are on quite different tracks. It is only with translations such as this that the twain might possibly meet.

Snow and Shadow, Dorothy Tse, Nicky Harman (trans.) (Muse Books, March 2014)

Running Through Beijing by Xu Zechen, translated by Eric Abrahamsen

reviewed by Peter Gordon

23 March 2014 — Dunhuang is a petty criminal (a trafficker in fake IDs) who has just been released from a short stint in prison. His partner is still inside and is he is deposited in Beijing in the middle of a sandstorm with nary a fen nor any connections or relationships.

This short novel, a mere 160 pages, is—like early Yu Hua—an exercise in realism rather than the magic realism or satire that is found in much contemporary Chinese literature. A translation of a 2006 novel (apparently called *Running Through Zhongguancun* in Chinese), *Running Through Beijing* features simple characters, simple situations, straightforward characterization and clear description with streaks of wry humor. The world of petty crime it describes—counterfeit CDs, part-time prostitution, clients who are as often as not students, four-to-a-room lodgings—is specifically Chinese. There is no exotica: this is a life of cigarettes, theft, police raids and living day-to-day, familiar to readers of fiction in its broad brush strokes if not the details.

Dunhuang leads his life after release in a state of bemusement. Immediately after being released, he is taken in by Xiaorong—a girl selling fake DVDs—out of a loneliness tinged with empathy. He partners with her and stays until her erstwhile boyfriend returns. The latter is none the wiser and supplies Dunhuang with counterfeit IDs from his larger operation. Under the impression that it was expected of him, Dunhuang then tracks down his previous and now incarcerated partner's girlfriend Qibao—no easy task since he had never met her, and all he knew was that she was also in the fake ID trade. Neither he nor Qibao respect her previous relationship, such as it was, for long: they all form a sort of ménage-a-quatre in both business and love.

Running Through Beijing—the title reflecting Dunhuang's habit of making his deliveries by jogging after a "second-hand" bicycle is stolen after a single outing—tells a simple story and tells it well. There are undoubtedly many shades of deeper meaning—there is, as one might expect in any novel about a *demi-monde*, considerable social commentary—but none of it matters greatly.

Dunhuang, while street-smart in many ways, seems clueless about the rest of existence. His aspirations are modest; he is on the whole accepting of life's complexities. While unschooled—to put it mildly—in the ways of love and women, he shows unexpected streaks of tenderness toward the women whose lives cross his. Xiaorong, older than him by a few years, is alternatively a lover, older sister and friend. Qibao, the other love interest, is a true *demi-mondaine*.

Dunhaung finds his purpose in life in a flash in the last few pages of the book.

The author Xu Zechen was unknown to me, but he comes with something of a pedigree. He is editor at *People's Literature* magazine and was selected for the University of Iowa's International Writing Program.

And this is a fine novel. One need not know or care more about Beijing to appreciate the humanity of its characters nor to be propelled through the story than one needs to know or care about the St. Petersburg of Dostoevsky. The foreignness of the setting and situation rapidly fades into the subconscious. I suspect, although one never knows, that the translator Eric Abrahamsen is to thank for at least of some of this. Abrahamsen has, through simplicity of language and use of terms like "the rat bastard" managed to retain a slight foreignness of tone, while delivering a fluent English text.

It's a cliché to say that a novel deserves to be read. *But if Running Through Beijing* is read, it is likely to be enjoyed.

Running Through Beijing, Xu Zechen,Eric Abrahamsen (trans) (Two Lines Press, May 2013)

Open Verdict: A Hong Kong Story by Ken Bridgewater

reviewed by Nigel Collett

29 January 2014 — On 15 January 1980, a large posse of Hong Kong policemen broke into a flat in the Government quarters at Ho Man Tin and found the body of a twenty-nine year old Scottish Police Inspector, John MacLennan. He was lying in a locked, pitch-black bedroom with four bullet holes in his chest and one bullet hole in his abdomen. By his body was his service revolver, which appeared to have been the weapon used to kill him, and on his desk lay a suicide note written on the back of an envelope. The police assumed that he had killed himself. They did not bother to conduct a proper forensic investigation and the body was hastily cremated. They and the Government were taken aback when the inquest jury refused to accept that the death was suicide, and returned an open verdict.

What followed was a public outcry led by the redoubtable Elsie Elliott (who, after her marriage, became the Elsie Tu most of us will recognize) and aided by the Commercial Radio chat show, Aileen Bridgewater. The Hong Kong Government was forced to yield to public pressure and, on 8 July 1980, appointed a Commission of Inquiry under Justice TL Yang, who delivered his report in 1981, giving his opinion that MacLennan had indeed committed suicide. Unfortunately, the evidence heard in the Inquiry and the extraordinary events surrounding it made it clear that the investigation had, at best, been mishandled and that MacLennan was, at the time of his death, the victim of an attempt to hound him out of the police force. This was being conducted by the Special Investigation Unit, the notorious SIU, which had ostensibly been set up to weed out homosexuals. It was also clear that the Government very much wanted the public to believe that the death was a suicide and that it, or some of its organs, or both, were prepared to go as far as discrediting or intimidating anyone who publicly questioned the verdict of suicide.

By its behaviour, the Government managed to taint the Inquiry report, and so the story of John MacLennan's death was felt by many to have been left unresolved. One of these was Ken Bridgewater, husband of broadcaster Aileen, who had been involved in helping his wife collect information about the case from the start of her involvement. Aileen was one of those whom agents of the Government had tried to intimidate; she blew the threats back at them by reading them out on the radio. The Bridgewaters accommodated John Conway, the private investigator appointed by the MacLennan family to represent them at the Inquiry and so were party to many of his discoveries (unlike the Inquiry, which refused to hear them—the Government managed to discredit Conway and to bar his evidence). Ken Bridgewater's access to detailed information was, therefore, unusually good.

Both Aileen and John Conway subsequently wrote of their views about the MacLennan case and about the pressure that was brought to bear upon them during it, Aileen in Chapter 23 of her 1983 memoirs *Talk of Hong Kong*, Conway in Chapter 2 of his 1994 book, *Speak for the Dead*. Now Ken Bridgewater has written a fictionalized account of the full story, "fictionalized", though, only to a very minor degree, for most of the story in his novel *Open Verdict* is either fact or assumptions based on fact. He appears in it himself as Kevin, and employs a few other pseudonyms when he needs to. Otherwise, the riveting story he unfolds is much as it happened forty-four years ago.

That does not mean that this book fails to read like a novel, for it does. The pace is fast, the dialogue rings true and the result is an exciting page-turner. Mirroring Aileen's radio exposures at the time of the case, the novel pulls no punches and will be an embarrassing read for some of the protagonists who are still alive, as many are. The Attorney General of the day, Mr John Griffiths, QC, does not emerge well from the story, though it is likely that the embarrassment which he may feel was a result of the instructions of the Governor, Sir Murray MacLehose, under which he was forced to operate. The Governor's presence and influence loomed behind the MacLennan affair, and his motivations and actions have never have been explained. He took whatever secrets he knew to the grave in 2000.

Why should this case fascinate so much even now? MacLennan seems to have been bisexual but whatever happened to him did so because the illegality of homosexuality at the time made any gay or bisexual policeman vulnerable to pressure. This made it absolutely clear that the law had to be changed, so the Yang Commission's report led directly to the Law Reform Commission's examination of the subject and their report of 1983. That, after a delay of eight years, led to the decriminalization of homosexuality in Hong Kong in 1991. The case has a rightful place in Hong Kong history.

The MacLennan case also has much to say about the nature of colonial society in Hong Kong. Some tend nowadays to look back with nostalgia at the "golden age" that is supposed to have existed here before the handover to China in 1997. The MacLennan case makes it clear that such a concept of recent history is illusory. The Hong Kong it uncovers is shot through with the high level misuse of power, vice, triad infiltration, police incompetence and corruption, murder, extortion, blackmail, violence and intimidation. The underbelly of the colony was black and control of it was exercised ruthlessly. The picture that emerges is disturbing, frightening even, given that many of those involved at the time, and who were not exposed then, must still be here.

Open Verdict concludes by asking the reader for his or her verdict on the case. Ken Bridgewater has his own ideas, and makes them clear, but he leaves enough space for doubt. It may never be known whether John MacLellan did kill himself or was murdered, but Ken Bridgewater's new account of his death and its aftermath leaves no doubt that he has never received justice.

Open Verdict: A Hong Kong Story, Ken Bridgewater (Trafford Press, December 2013)

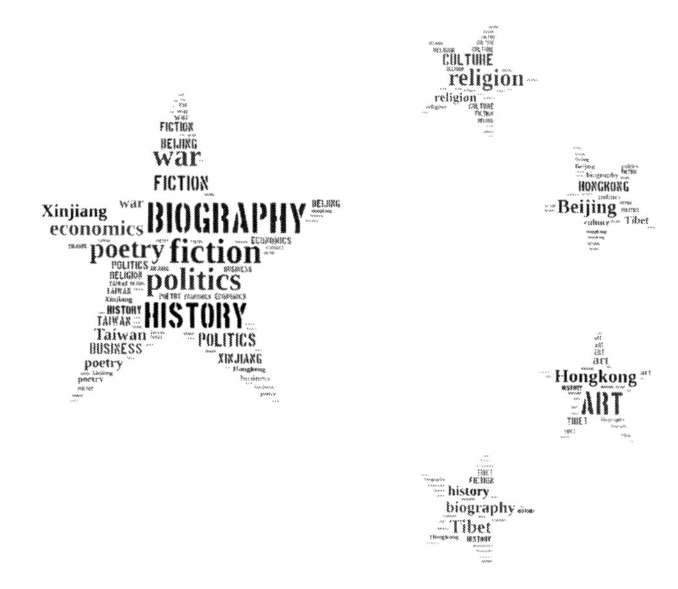
FICTION
BEIJING
war
FICTION
Xinjiang
war
BIOGRAPHY
BEIJING
economics
poetry
fiction
ECONOMICS
POLITICS
RELIGION
politics
BUSINESS
HISTORY
TAIWAN
HISTORY
Taiwan
POLITICS
BUSINESS
XINJIANG
poetry
CULTURE
religion
religion
CULTURE
HONGKONG
Beijing
Tibet
Hongkong
ART
history
biography
Tibet

Poetry

Desde Hong Kong: Poets in conversation with Octavio Paz, edited by Germán Muñoz, Tammy Ho Lai-ming and Juan José Morales

reviewed by Henry Wei Leung

18 November 2014 — *Desde Hong Kong* must be the first of its kind: a Hong Kong poetry anthology in English which is not topically on Hong Kong. The book celebrates the occasion of Octavio Paz's centenary, putting its poets in conversation with his work and legacy. Conversation: not perspective, not reportage, not sightseeing. This means a book with almost no trace of gawkers writing in a shop-worn East-meets-West English-with-an-accent diversity rhetoric. This means English poems which channel-switch with Cantonese and Mandarin as much as with Spanish, Tagalog, and Hebrew. This means a turn in Hong Kong poetics, in which no apology is made for its existence and the landscape becomes inner.

Paz's place in the anthology and what bearing he might have upon a Hong Kong literature are worth further exploration. He was eminently cosmopolitan, yes, and the influence of "Eastern" poetics on his work was profound (consider how his prosody benefited from Basho's choza de sílabas), yes, but moreover he was a writer keenly aware of the unwarranted imposition of national histories on literary histories. Some of his essays speak especially to language's necessary reinventions of itself. English and its literary traditions occupy a peculiar space in Hong Kong, a post-colony with clear borders and some definite national characteristics but which is not a country of its own. These words from Paz's 1964 essay "The Siren and the Seashell"[1], might illuminate the politics of a Hong Kong English literary tradition:

> To be a contemporary of Goethe or Tamerlane is a coincidence, happy or otherwise, in which one's will plays no part; to desire to be their contem-

> porary implies a will to participate, intellectually, in the actions of history, to share a history that belongs to others but that one somehow makes one's own. It is an affinity and a distance—and an awareness of that situation. The Modernists did not want to be French: they wanted to be modern.

Mani Rao's multitextual poem, "I Talk to Myself — I Talk to You," opens *Desde Hong Kong* and speaks exactly to this affinity and distance. The poem is an arrangement of quotations which puts several writers into conversation across eras and languages. She begins with Paz:

> Man is inhabited by silence and space
>
> ...
>
> How to escape my own image?

The Marquis de Sade answers, via the accounting of Madame de Saint-Ange, via another layer of translators:

> By repeating our attitudes and postures in a thousand different ways, they infinitely multiply those same pleasures ... these images are so many groups disposed around those enchained by love ...

Celan then enters the dialogue, and then others, and others. The poem closes on a wistful note from one of Hong Kong's beloveds, the recently deceased Leung Ping-kwan, just as the lines begin to break open into white space. Rao gets the last word, in a footnote, in which her remarks on the sources directly address the reader:

> And PK Leung who no longer meets you and me for dinner in Hong Kong joins us in the response.

The poem is thus an elegy of voices long gone and recently gone, an intimacy by invocation. It sets a gorgeous tone of inwardness for the rest of the anthology, in which the subject is both *I* and *we*, yet neither fully *I* nor fully *we*.

* * *

What is marvelous about these poems is the way they start to trace a common language. By this I don't mean English. An idiom develops from the lines of Paz's "Between Going and Staying", "Sunstone" and others, which are obvious inspirations to the poems at hand. Consider Michellan Alagao's poem which begins in universals,

> Your forever arriving
> is my never-ending goodbye:
> y llega siempre, walang hanggang paalam;

only to backpedal with a warning: "both with things lost in translation."

But, in each case of Alagao's smoothly slipping into other languages—none of them estranged by italicization—we see how much is also gained in translation. Consider, as another example, Tammy Ho Lai-Ming's sonnet whose "I give, and I give, and I give" leads into the refrain, "the pattern's not undone", which crescendos in a final unraveling: "Of primitive earth, pealed bare." The homophone there (I'm inclined not to read it as a typo) gives us the sense of a bell pealing: layers of sound contracting inward in order to expand outward, which resonates deeply with the poem's intimations of motherhood. Peeling, but also pealing. Consider also Jason Eng Hun Lee's poem which replants Paz's *árbol adentro* in a Romantic's urban sea:

> Here, each tree comprises its own island,
> and each man is his own castaway.
>
> Yet I harbor a secret that none
> shall take away from me –

Paz wrote, in a 1961 essay calling nationalism "an aesthetic fallacy", that "Literature is broader than frontiers." When we read Nicholas YB Wong's "If We Are a Metaphor of the Universe", an anaphoric list poem trapped in the first part of the subjunctive, do we read the "we" as representing what appears to be Hong Kong? Or an anonymous city? Or citizens? Or modern humanity? It is a poem of deep ambivalence, helplessness, and pride, and it speaks multitudes:

> If a frog in a well knows it has swum in creeks as a tadpole, unashamed
> If the well suddenly wants to travel but what to take with its hollow torso

These are images coming from a deep privacy. I cannot avoid mentioning that *Desde Hong Kong*'s publication coincides, extraordinarily, with the city's ongoing protests which have also seen an efflorescence of artistic expression. What does poetry, in English, in conversation with a Spanish poet of a gone generation, have to do with this urgent local crisis? Profound questions of national identity have been raised and refracted by the protests, and this poetry offers one answer: not the development of a national language, but rather of a private language, plural, to render the inner life rich with meaning.

* * *

What I see Paz teaching the poets in this anthology is the immateriality of home. Trish Hopkinson's poem asks:

> Is this path the poem — the journey
> hat dissolves into nothingness?

Such a nothingness is not absence, nor is it mere subtraction. It is the way

> the shadow of Splendor recites verse
> more naked than herself.

It is James Shea's "Firsthand Account of Myself" in images of stillness, his tracing backward to find that

> single forgiveness
> built into the sin.

It is Douglas Robinson quoting Paz on the translation of a foreign tongue into one's own

to restore
the unity
of the beginning.

As concerns the perennial identity politics of Hong Kong's literature in English, the makeup of this anthology's poets is especially inclusive, embracing this notion that translation—an outward-moving positive creation—doesn't take us farther from the source but closer. Indeed, the anthology's closing poem is the translation from Chinese of a Wang Jiaxin poem, whose

emptiness and ash —
all crackling in a fire
come late in life

is one of the most poignant images of Paz and his legacy.

Not all the poems included are mature, and some of the poets may be more identifiably "Hong Kong" than others. But to my reading it is significant that, for the most part, the poetics is cohesive.

It should be no surprise that many of these poems allude to or cite Paz's "Between Going and Staying". The anthology's poetics is bound up in longing, loss, and drift. Would you expect otherwise from a city-state which has no citizenship, only a residency status quantified by years? What we're presented with is not just "Hong Kong" but *desde* or from Hong Kong—a preposition already on the move. Read Jennifer Wong's poem to see what I mean, and Madeleine Slavick's, and Hao Guang Tse's, and many others. Better yet, read them all.

Notes
[1] All translations of Paz's essays are by Lysander Kemp and Margaret Sayers Peden.

Desde Hong Kong: Poets in conversation with Octavio Paz, Germán Muñoz, Juan José Morales and Tammy Ho Lai-Ming (eds.) (Chameleon Press, September 2014)

Something Crosses My Mind by Wang Xiaoni, translated by Eleanor Goodman

reviewed by Jennifer Wong

16 August 2014 — Translating Wang Xiaoni's work is no easy task, given Wang's unusual, complex imagery and introspective language, and yet Eleanor Goodman has rendered it beautifully in the newly-launched book *Something Crosses My Mind*. By opting for a pared-down, faithful translation that respects the nature of Chinese language and poetic metaphors, this bilingual collection captures Wang's poetic imagination and inventiveness as a poet as well as facilitates appreciation of the stylistics of contemporary Chinese poetry.

In the translator's foreword, she sets out a major challenge of this project:

> In the world of contemporary Chinese poetry, Wang Xiaoni's work cannot be neatly fit into any of the most fashionable categories... She is not interested in imitating T S Eliot or Li Bai.

The difficulty in nailing down Wang's writing style illustrates her strength as a poet. Her metaphorical language is incisive and layered with multiple meanings. Eleanor Goodman sees Wang as "a poet of place". Born in Jilin, Wang has lived in northeast China as well as in Shenzhen and Hainan in southern China. Her poetry reflects a sense of belonging that rests in the mind rather than a geographical location, and a desire for meaningful existence instead of mere survival.

Despite being classified as a misty poet—a literary movement in China characterized by obscure, abstract metaphors with hidden meanings—although she steers away from the term herself. It is fairer to say that her poetry reflects day-to-day struggles in the modern Chinese society by suggesting the importance of thoughts. In “A Rag’s Betrayal”, the image of a spotless window is used as a metaphor for the poet’s exposed thoughts. The clarity of vision threatens her and makes her vulnerable, even though she acknowledges others’ right to stare at her:

> Other people’s greatest freedom
> is the freedom to see.

Immediately after, the poet surveys the surreal landscape of the city, juxtaposing the beautiful springtime (subjective and organic) with cubism (methodical and framed), highlighting her self-awareness of living in this surreal, fast-changing world.

> In this complex and beautiful springtime
> cubism walks across the canvas.

“At Night What’s Inside the Skyscrapers” presents the glamor and eerie atmosphere of the city at night. Uninhabited, urban developments appear soulless. Wang emphasizes the individual’s resolve to retreat into a private, peaceful world, although it is uncertain how far this escape from the urban threat can last:

> The skyscrapers are unbearably bright
> I take an eye-closing pill.
> In this life to be human is already glorious.

Goodman’s strength as a translator lies in her ability to render the Chinese poetic language faithfully and with elegance, adhering to syntax and line breaks, while taking care that the translated verse does not alienate the reader. She has kept true to Wang’s immediate, unaffected voice, and maintained her uncanny, pithy word choice. She also refrains from the temptation to over-translate or gloss over the strangeness of poetic language. A fuller annotation of terms might however benefit those readers unfamiliar with Chinese rituals, regional life and dialects. The decision to make this book a bilingual edition makes it possible for sinologists and those who are able to access both languages to compare and understand how Chinese and English poetic language and form operate.

In an interview with Wen Xue Bao, Wang remarks that she writes for herself rather than for the world. It is this open-mindedness to document life as it is that makes her work so mysterious and captivating. Despite her statement to the contrary, her work is full of energy and reflects the strangeness of the times in China, where people living in the city as well as those who are in the countryside are haunted by a feeling of alienation and the uncertainty of future.

Her work is also underpinned by a subdued, prose-like fluency that is neither masculine nor feminine. Goodman's translation interprets this well, often maintaining the slightly disconcerting rhythm in Wang's poetry. An example is the poem "The One Lifting a Lamp in Front of the Mud Hut", which captures the cadence of spoken Chinese:

> What does that mud hut have to illuminate
> what do the cobbled streets too narrow for a donkey have to illuminate
> what does the whole world have to illuminate.

To my delight, the book presents a substantial selection of Wang's writings over the past two decades, especially poems that reflect her attitude towards the contradictory laws of nature and society, and the incredible that almost escape our notice in the tedium of everyday life. Overall, this is an ambitious volume that exudes authenticity and intelligence. It highlights the inventive form and language in Wang's poetry, making it a very helpful text for the studies of contemporary Chinese poetry.

Something Crosses My Mind, Xiaoni Wang, Eleanor Goodman (trans) (Zephyr Press, August 2014; Chinese University Press, August 2014)

Ancestral Worship: Poems by David McKirdy

reviewed by Agnès Bun

14 May 2014 — The portrait of a city as an old flame: poet David McKirdy is a man in love. His second collection of poems, *Ancestral Worship*, is an ode to Hong Kong, where he moved at the tender age of four.

In this most recent work, he sketches the outline of the town, his town, where he still resides, and fills it with treasured memories: postcards from his life trimmed to poem size. Colorful characters walk by, such as an 82-year-old Indonesian shoe shiner, rickshaw coolies, sampan girls, with the signature scents of the town as an olfactive backdrop: Tiger Balm, fried spicy squids, sandalwood... Shadows of past settlers from the West and present tourists from Mainland China blend in the bustling streets he depicts.

Defining himself as an "Asian writer", McKirdy already reflected on his status as an *Accidental Occidental* in a first poetry collection published in 2005. In this book, he reiterates his feeling of being outlandish, estranged in his own birthplace in Europe, at home in the foreign Far East.

> I've got the blood of China in my veins
> not through father, mother or distant forebears
> but passed on from another's ancient line.
> — "*Ancestral Worship*"

There is no need to be familiar with Hong Kong to appreciate the verses. They are, after all, not so much about the city itself, but rather about how a man's soul can resonate with a foreign land, and how he decides to tie his fate to it.

Such a choice comes with its drawbacks. No matter how hard he tries, this self-professed "white ghost" knows that there is a double standard, and that he cannot entirely fit in, stuck in his social caste. He thus recalls his local childhood friend:

> We left home together for school
> you on foot
> me on the bus
> attending classes at either end of another street
> both burdened by the hopes and expectations
> of another generation.
> — "*Citizen Ship*"

These heavy considerations are fortunately balanced by lighter notes; McKirdy knows how to poke fun at himself.

> I speak Chinese badly, very well.
> — "*Speak Chinese*"

Others also bear the brunt of his wit and irony, such as the Mainland Chinese tourists:

> The short trip between Island and Mainland
> once a lifeline
> now the tee-shirt experience
> of a package tour
> in our world city.'
> —"*Star Struck*"

But behind this cheeky tone which pervades the whole book, a soft, sad whisper can be heard, mourning the loss of the city he once knew and cherished, as modernization creeps in.

The faint footfalls of those gone before.
What will we leave
as we sink into the past?
— "*Fragrant Harbour*"

The most poignant pieces are not however the ones dedicated to Hong Kong. McKirdy lost his parents while writing this book. Undoubtedly one of the most heart-wrenching, haunting poems is the one he dedicates to his father:

Later I bathed you
as you did me in infancy
a filial debt finally repaid.

and:

The day you died
the wind-damaged fence lost a board
and your flowers gave up the fight.
— "*Dying Flowers*"

And with McKirdy, outcast per conviction, emotional ties are not solely ones of blood. In his homage to his amah and her "mouth full of gold", he writes:

Ah May, Amah, Mama
fifty years on the shadow of your presence remains
as the wax from the candle I light for you
rolls down

like tears.
— "*Amah*"

This is McKirdy at its best: quiet and elegant free verse, used to convey the most powerful emotions. Should he mourn or celebrate? He decides to do both, with simplicity, as his poems resuscitate ghosts from the past in their whole benevolent glory.

As a collection, *Ancestral Worship* pays tribute, unconditionally, to the power of memory, to overcome loss, grief, and the ability of words to remember and revive, whether the shadow of a cherished city, or the silhouette of deceased loved ones.

McKirdy's nostalgic voice is definitely worth listening to, as he contours the canvas of the city he loves so dearly, at home in the world of his memories.

Ancestral Worship, David McKirdy (Chameleon Press, May 2014)

on can be obtained at www.ICGtesting.com
A
31214
'00003B/6/P

About the *Asian Review*

The only pan-Asian publication
Review of Books is available on-li
and tablets and in regular print
online booksellers.

asianreviewofboo

The *Asian Review of Books* in print:

Volume 1, Number 1: July 2014 ISBN 978-988-18
Volume 1, Number 2: October 2014 ISBN 978-988-13
Volume 1, Number 3: January 2015 ISBN 978-988-13

CPSIA informa
Printed in the U
BVOW01s2019
379556B